C U R R E N C Y

D O U B L E D A Y

LIVING
WITHOUT A
GOAL

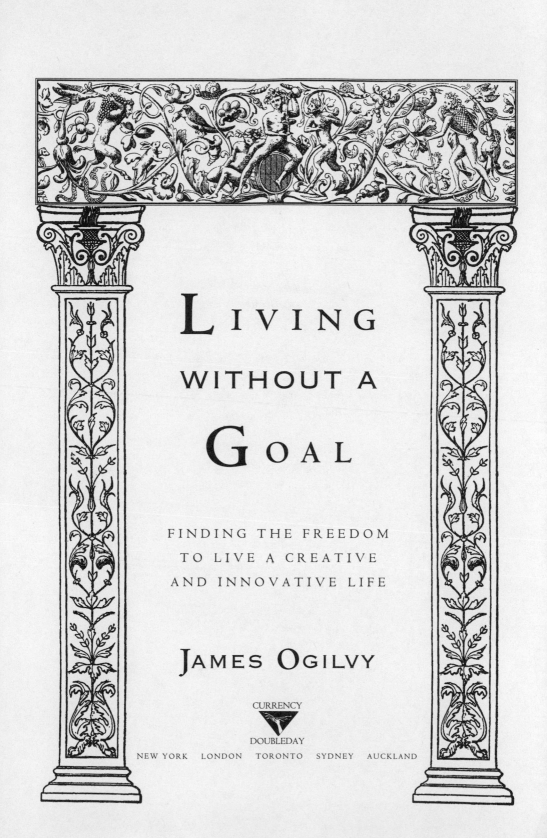

LIVING WITHOUT A GOAL

FINDING THE FREEDOM TO LIVE A CREATIVE AND INNOVATIVE LIFE

JAMES OGILVY

CURRENCY
DOUBLEDAY

NEW YORK   LONDON   TORONTO   SYDNEY   AUCKLAND

A Currency Book
PUBLISHED BY DOUBLEDAY
a division of Bantam Doubleday Dell Publishing Group, Inc.
1540 Broadway, New York, New York 10036

CURRENCY and DOUBLEDAY are trademarks of Doubleday, a division of Bantam
Doubleday Dell Publishing Group, Inc.

BOOK DESIGN BY CAROL MALCOLM RUSSO/SIGNET M DESIGN, INC.

Library of Congress Cataloging-in-Publication Data
Ogilvy, James A.
Living without a goal : finding the freedom to live a creative and
innovative life / James Ogilvy. — 1st ed.
p.   cm.
"A Currency book"—T.p. verso.
Includes bibliographical references.
1. Life.   2. Creative ability.   3. Self-actualization (psychology)
I. Title.
BD435.O34   1995
128—dc20   94-29030
                                                           CIP

ISBN 0-385-41799-3

CONTENTS

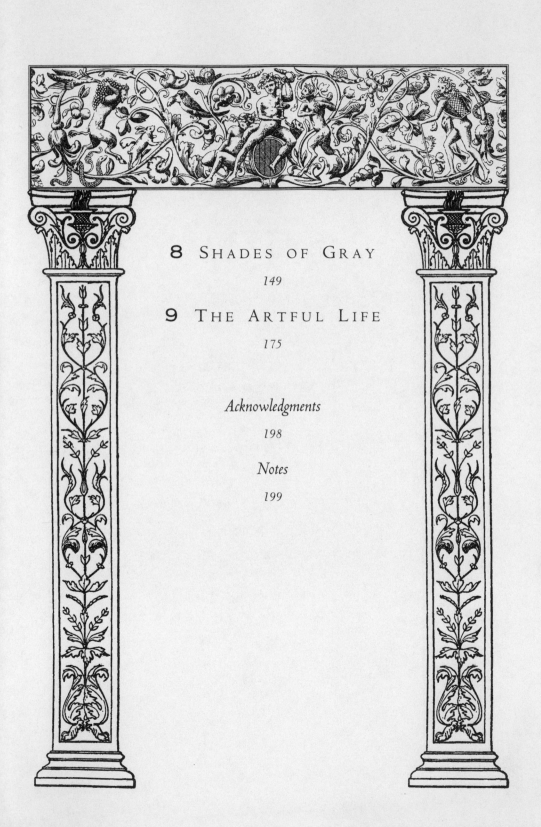

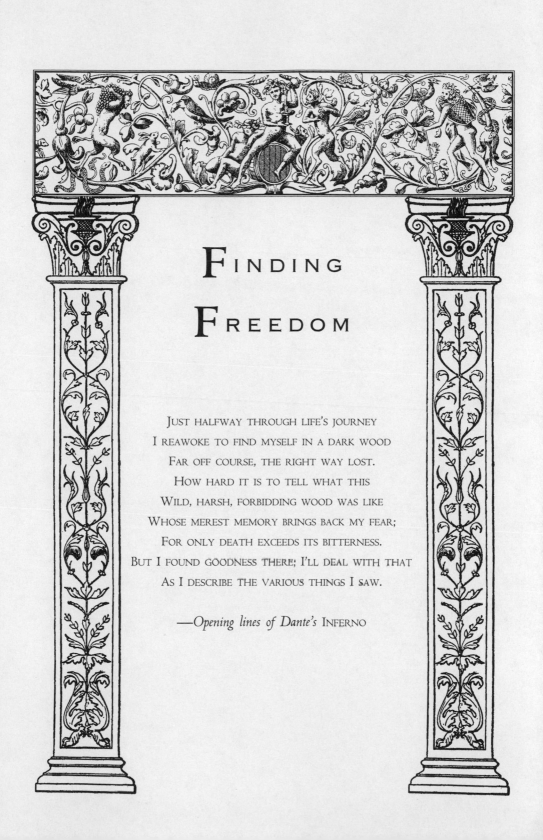

FINDING FREEDOM

Just halfway through life's journey
I reawoke to find myself in a dark wood
Far off course, the right way lost.
How hard it is to tell what this
Wild, harsh, forbidding wood was like
Whose merest memory brings back my fear;
For only death exceeds its bitterness.
But I found goodness there; I'll deal with that
As I describe the various things I saw.

—*Opening lines of Dante's* INFERNO

1

 DID NOT HAVE TO WAIT FOR A
midlife crisis to find myself lost in a dark
wood. The first of several departures
from the quest for a goal came when I
was just sixteen. I was seated behind the wheel of a 1947
Mercury convertible, wind whipping through my hair, driving
into a black night and a future darker than any I had ever seen.
I had just been expelled from boarding school.

Suddenly I had been relieved of my future. I had failed to
live up to the goals that had been set for me. Now what?
College? Would any good college have me? Had I fallen forever
off life's great ladder? Was I permanently disqualified from the
race? I had no idea. I was frightened. I had messed up. I had
disappointed my parents. I should have felt awful, but instead,

just as Dante "found goodness" behind his fear, I felt an odd and unexpected glow of excitement, exhilaration: a sense of life lived in real time.

Rather than weeping from the experience of loss and failure, I felt a sudden and unexpected sense of release. This first flush of Goallessness felt like a liberation from a future that was all too well defined: prep school, college, profession. As I sped through miles of darkness down Route 101 across southern New Hampshire, my hi-beams could not penetrate the core of mystery in front of me. Because I did not know where I was going, I was making it up as I went along, and it felt more like living than following a rule book for life. But I can say this only in hindsight. At the time I was frightened and confused at the conflict between fear and exhilaration. What would become of me? Had I destroyed the life that had seemed to stretch out so clearly and gloriously in front of me toward the shining goal of Success?

It has taken me some time to sort out that youthful confusion between fear and exhilaration. Once upon a time I hoped to figure out this puzzle called life. When I finally got to college I majored in philosophy, then taught it for a dozen years. I never did figure out the purpose of my life. That great blueprint in the sky that philosophy seemed to promise was never revealed to me. Maybe mathematics holds some timeless truths, but when it comes to human history, we're making it up as we go along, and we don't always get it right. So how do we figure out what to do from one day to the next?

All around me I see people pursuing various grand overriding Goals: Wealth, Love, Fame, Religious Salvation, Social Justice, Self-actualization, Wisdom . . . I have come to believe that a life enslaved to a single Goal, no matter how noble, becomes a mechanism rather than an organism, a business plan rather than a biography, a tool rather than a gift.

I will refer to those Grand Goals that enslave by using capital letters to mock their pretension to personal destinies. Living without a Goal does not require us to abandon all goals. When you go down to the corner to get a newspaper, you have a goal. When you have a curable form of cancer, you have a goal: health. Scientists live with the goal of discovery. Throwing off the burden of poverty is a goal. Doctors, poets and obsessed geniuses receive callings that impose legitimate goals. But many of us suffer neither the burdens of poverty nor the lure of a calling. No goal has been *given* to us, but somehow we think we should *find* one.

Following Dante, many people first confront Goallessness in midlife. Youth is filled with goals: get through school, find a mate, get a decent job and a comfortable place to live, make a difference, accomplish something. But after one has accomplished something, attained a few goals, then what? Midlife confronts many of us with the nagging suspicion that we missed our destinies, and then we cast about for some Goal more noble than any we have achieved to date. But midlife is not the only time one can get lost in a dark wood, as I discovered at sixteen. And I suspect there are many who rode the escalator of ambition during the eighties and now, well short of midlife, are finding that upward mobility can be habit forming. This book is about breaking the habit of overweening ambition —at any age.

There is no escaping some goal-directed behavior, and it is not my intention to *extol* Goallessness or recommend it as the *right* way to live. For those of us who lack an undeniable calling, Goallessness is our condition, like it or not. It is not something you are *supposed* to learn. It is not something you *ought to be.* Least of all can you set Goallessness as your Goal. How self-contradictory that would be! But I do want to question that nagging suspicion that you *ought* to have a Grand Goal that defines the purpose of your life. That nagging suspicion is a hangover from an age when religious or political absolutes defined the rules of the game of life, and a clear goal line, e.g., the pearly gates of heaven, defined the meaning of success. But now that the old absolutes have lost their credibility (see Chapter 3), many of us find ourselves playing games with no goal lines. What counts as success? Which direction to run? Where are the authorities who would tell us? There are none to be found. So we sometimes seek in odd places for replacements to the Goals we have lost. Rather than engaging in a vain attempt to replace the old absolutes, however, this book is about living with, even rejoicing in, the loss. A life with a single Grand Goal robs you of your freedom, because a life devoted to a single Goal demands that every action serve that single end.

THIS BOOK IS about designing life artistically rather than engineering life mechanically. Artistic design calls for freedom and spontaneity where engineering builds upon the laws of mechanical necessity. Many of us use Grand Goals to deny our own freedom. We allow ourselves to become the slaves of our Goals. You know the story. Get up in the morning. Go to work. You confront the tasks in front of you. You experience each moment as a means to the next. One job leads to another. You become the tool of your tasks. This is slavery, not freedom.

Slaves are chained to the goals of their masters. Many of us think we are free because we are not, technically speaking, slaves. We have not been bought on the slave trader's block. We are free to run away any time we want. Or are we? We do not run away. What holds us? Our Goals. However exhilarating freedom can be, we are afraid to surrender those navigational aids that could steer us out of Dante's dark wood.

Goals and purposes are so good for giving direction to a life. They are such good organizers of actions. Single-mindedness, for what it's worth, becomes possible. With a single Goal shining like a beacon on the horizon, navigation is easy: just aim for that point source of light and full steam ahead.

Somehow there must be a way of raising one's sights toward larger ambitions than the pleasure of the moment and the company of a few friends. But every attempt at justifying a particular ambition by hooking it to some grand vision of progress has been justly undermined in these postmodern times. I take it that both God and Karl Marx are dead, and that the passionate pursuit of religious salvation or political revolution is now a quaint relic of the past. Some readers will strongly disagree. For those still seeking the kingdom of God on earth, Goallessness is not a problem. To those ideologically committed comrades striving to bring about a classless society I say, "You are fortunate in your misfortune: you may never succeed in your quest, but at least you have the good fortune of having a quest to guide your path."

For the rest of us, for all those who (with an occasional reminder) can see through the purported finality of that time-honored quest for an all-consuming Goal, our problem is figuring out how to live once we have been relieved of that beacon on the horizon. How then do we navigate?

Lacking ultimate Goals as navigational aids, one runs into

two sorts of problems, one that is superficial and obvious, the other, fairly subtle. The first is the familiar experience of being lost. You can't figure out how to get where you want to go because you don't know where you are. The second is more insidious: it's not just the inability to get where you want to go; it's having no place to go. Confusion about how to get where you are going is one thing, utter aimlessness another. Aimlessness can feel like nihilism. Nothing is quite worth doing.

These problems with Goallessness are enough to make most people grasp for an overriding Goal. You feel that if only you could find the purpose of your life you could escape the confusion of aimlessness. But when you try to identify *the use* of your entire life, you are asking to be *used*. When you try to identify *the function* of your entire life, you are asking to be turned into a mere *functionary*.

The *useful* self, in thrall to some external Goal, is little more than a cog in the vast industrial machine, a means to some end not of its own making. Rather than an industrial paradigm that sees the self as a "human resource," as a means to an end, or as a tool for producing some external Goal, we would do better to seek an artistic paradigm.

Beauty is an end in itself, not a means to some other end. Art serves no other end, which is why attempts to nail down the *function* of art are fruitless. Likewise the free individual is one who serves her own ends rather than the ends of another. And she may do so without being selfish or narcissistic. If she sets self-gratification or self-realization as her Goal, then selfish she will be. But the artful creation of a self in real time, without a blueprint or a plan, lies at the heart of what I mean by "living without a Goal." How to tell the difference between a life aimed toward the Goal of self-realization and artfully living without a Goal? Sorting out this fairly subtle distinction will take more than a few chapters.

THE RHYTHM OF this book falls into three main movements. Following a few more introductory pages that define the difference between goals and Goals, Chapter 3 reviews some of the Goals that have preoccupied the baby boomers, from social justice and religious salvation to the psychological Goal of self-actualization. For many boomers and others as well, social and political Goals were put aside for the psychological Goal of self-actualization. This turn from outer Goals to inner Goals is the theme of this book's second movement.

Self-actualization was always a legitimate goal for a few: kings and aristocrats mostly. There has always been an opportunity for a few souls to experience the joys of self-creation or the sorrows of existential despair. But now the secret is out and great hordes of people are crowding into the psyche's workshop. Call it the democratization of identity or the trickling down of neurosis. It comes with the dawning of self-consciousness in more and more of the species, a waking of the sleepwalkers, an animation of what had previously been little more than biological automata. Call it the freeing of the slaves. Call it, as Tom Wolfe does, "a Happiness Explosion . . . ego extension, the politics of pleasure, the self-realization racket, the pharmacology of Overjoy." Some call it narcissism and brand it today's leading form of mental illness.

Call it, as Hegel did, a process of *coming to,* of becoming oneself *(werden zu sich)*. Listen to Nietzsche's Zarathustra repeat his incantation: "Become who you are!" Hear Socrates cite the words over the entry to the temple of the oracle at Delphi: "Know thyself." Recall Carl Jung's endless tracts devoted to the process of *individuation:* the gradual or sometimes sudden discovery of one's own principle of individuation *(principium individuationis).*

All these versions of the message in all these languages have particular wrinkles to them. Each has its own principle of individuation that makes each philosophy sound just a little bit different from the next. But there is also a common drift that they share. Somehow each of these thinkers, sages, psychologists and philosophers is saying to his readers and hearers, "Don't come to me for a Goal. It's up to you. You must find your own way. You must find out who you are." It sounds so simple . . . this Goal of self-actualization.

But of course it is *not* altogether simple because there can be costs to the awakening of consciousness. For society there are problems of crowd control. Automata are much easier to regiment if you have easy access to their control panels. It's easy to get slaves to march in step, but organizing a pack of self-motivated anarchists is harder than herding cats.

For the individual there are also costs: the loss of a sense of solidarity, loneliness, an anxiety over the lack of a clear sense of direction. Jean Paul Sartre captured the anxiety of Goallessness in a lovely phrase, "the vertigo of freedom." He also wrote, "Man is a useless passion." Most readers took this as a statement of pessimistic despair. To the contrary, I interpret Sartre's charge of uselessness as an eloquent statement of the essence of freedom.

The turn from social Goals to self-actualization might look

like the abandonment of adolescent Goals for the sake of the more modest goals of adulthood. But the same single-minded passion and fervor we directed toward society in the sixties we then poured into ourselves in the seventies, shrewdly labeled "The Me Decade" by Tom Wolfe. Rather than our achieving Goallessness, the cultivation of the precious self became our Goal, and social critics were soon complaining about creeping narcissism. Chapters 4 and 5 follow this book's second movement, from those outer Goals of the sixties to the inner Goal of the seventies. Somewhere between the "Summer of Love" in 1967 and the loveless narcissism of the seventies, there must be a third way. Chapters 6 through 8 sort out the subtleties of sublimation in order to describe a Goalless love that is neither self-absorbed nor so romantic as to be unsustainable. In order to penetrate the mysteries of sublime love, the third movement links erotic sublimation to the sublimation of the economy: the move from the industrial to the information era.

Following the third movement on erotic and economic sublimation, the coda, Chapter 9, points toward the sublimity of Goallessness in "The Artful Life." Living without a Goal is like creating a work of art in the sense that artistic creativity serves no goal outside itself. A work of art may have an impact, but that is not *why* it was created. Artistic creativity is not beholden to goals in the way engineering is. An engineer has a job to do, and will assemble the tools and means to do it. An artist may be driven by some dream of the perfect artwork, but the act of creation is filled with moments of free choice that are not as prescribed by necessity as the engineer's calculations.

RUNNING THROUGHOUT THIS book is a leitmotif—the background of shifting historical epochs, from the agricultural era, through the industrial era, to today's information era. Industrial technology is a vast construction of instruments and means for the efficient production of end products to serve our wants and needs. Goallessness represents an alternative to an instrumental rationality that insists on seeing all action as a means toward some end or goal. The alternative to instrumental rationality is a more affective sensitivity less intent on *manipulating* the world than on *appreciating* it.

Whatever mistakes we have made in our desecration of nature, we had good reasons for becoming clever at manipulating our physical environment. The struggle for survival in the face of harsh necessity demanded that we get good at manipulating the physics and chemistry of the physical world. Efficiency and productivity were legitimate measures to use in evaluating the means to the ends of survival. But once we learned to use these measures in their legitimate domain, we acquired mental habits that we then extend—illegitimately—to other domains, like human freedom, art, symbolism or humor.

In order to understand ourselves at the dawn of the information era, we need to abandon a vocabulary that was mainly adapted to manipulating means toward ends in mechanics and engineering—words like "material," "marginal utility," "efficiency" and "productivity." We need to adopt a new vocabulary, a new set of concepts drawn from art and information theory—words like "sublime," "spontaneity," "creativity" and "marginal intensity." Signs and symbols are not to be understood through physics and engineering. Neither are people. As fruitless wrangles over freedom and determinism during the industrial era have demonstrated, one cannot expect to make sense of freedom using the categories of the industrial toolmaker's instrumental rationality.

The condition of Goallessness and the condition of the artist share a similar rhythm, a similar attitude toward time. Real time. Not the turnover of rote mechanical sequence, but the suspense and opportunity of the unexpected. Goallessness is not a matter of "living for today for tomorrow we may die." Real time does not stop with the present. Real time has a future. The frozen present exists only in the phony existentialism of beer commercials. Real time has a long tail called history, and in front of its nose stretch far more than one path into the unknown. Real time is irrevocable. Mistakes can be made. Successes can be achieved. And nothing, absolutely nothing, is guaranteed, not the morning paper, not the mail delivery, not love. Today's future is so profoundly unknown, so ineffable, so largely unpredictable.

Grand Goals with names like Destiny belie the structure of real time. They treat the future as if it had the determinacy of the past. Not even the past is fully determinate. The present's tail has a way of swishing with each reinterpretation, each new significance added by our daily actions. But at least the past is more determinate than the future. At least it gives us something approaching facts.

Living without a Goal requires neither the optimism of a secure future nor the pessimism of hopelessness. Goallessness is neither a matter of counting on the promise of better days to come nor abandoning hopes of same. Things might get better; they might not. Who can tell? Living without a Grand Goal while orchestrating many goals offers opportunities for free choice, design, intelligence, play. Thriving in real time takes work, leavened with a vivid sense of play.

THIS BUSINESS OF work and play will be a recurrent theme. Too much of our work amounts to the drudgery of arranging means toward ends, mechanically placing the right foot in front of the left and the left in front of the right, moving down narrow corridors toward narrow goals. Play widens the halls. Work will always be with us, and many works are worthy. But the worthiest works of all often reflect an artful creativity that looks more like play than work.

Consider musical improvisation, artists at work, tasks that call for creativity. You don't always know exactly where you'll end when you start. You don't always have a clear goal. Think of the foolishness of the question: What is the purpose of play?

Praise of play sounds frivolous. The very idea of living without a Goal smacks of luxury. But as more and more of America's menial jobs move offshore or succumb to automation, the work that remains demands higher levels of mindful creativity. There are fewer rewards for following standard procedures, fewer opportunities for human automata. A capacity for innovation is as important in an information economy as the need for standardization was important to the industrial economy. But innovation is the very opposite of standardization, as different as the production of the *different* is from the mass production of the *same, same, same.*

The less menial and mechanical a job is, the more playfulness and creativity will have a role in its completion. The artfulness of living without a Goal can serve the goals of work by bringing creativity and freedom to what otherwise would be drudgery and enslavement.

As I approach the paradox of useful uselessness—or the goal of Goallessness—I have the sorry sense of trying to explain a joke. Putting play to work gets as tricky as working at play. Beware the forced joviality of the company picnic. There is something sad about people who insist on the usefulness of play. They bring to their play the rigor and regimentation they need in their work. You see them in sweat clubs clenching their jaws to the sound of clanking Nautilus machines. But the useful tedium of exercise is the very opposite of the useless, playful passion at the heart of freedom.

The useful self is always at work. The free self knows how to play. The line between useful work and useless play is not hard and fast. As refugees of bureaucracies know all too well, some work is useless. And play has its uses: recreation, relaxation, learning. But, like art, play is for the most part an end in itself. And purposeful work has its virtues.

There is always work to be done. Each job will have its goals, its tasks, and its own set of useful tools. It would be foolish to purge ourselves of the entire vocabulary of goal-directed action. But the preoccupations of the industrial era—with technique and technology, with utility, productivity and efficiency—are not the most appropriate preoccupations for steering an entire life, especially when more and more of that life is lived in the symbolic economy of the information era.

BEFORE DESCRIBING IN greater detail just what I *do* mean by Goallessness, I'd like to say what I *don't* mean, to narrow the range of possibilities by sorting out forms of goallessness that are indefensible. Let us therefore construct a short catalog of the kinds and varieties of Goallessness, with a few comments on their varying degrees of (un)acceptability.

1. IMPULSIVENESS

Some choose not to deal with goals at all but to exist entirely as creatures of impulse. In *The Executioner's Song*, Norman Mailer's literary docudrama about Gary Gilmore, a confessed killer, Mailer portrays the immediacy and impulsiveness of Gilmore's actions. How short the loop from desire to gratification in Gilmore's world! Thirsty? Want some beer? To hell with the long chain of linkages from desire, through realization of a lack, to labor for reward and purchase using the fruits of labor and its reward. Instead: there's beer on the shelf of the nearest 7-11. Grab it, and shoot the guy behind the counter if he objects. Bam! Next? The tyranny of impulse leads to a myopia of the moment. If you cannot see beyond the present instant and its hungers, you risk ending up on death row.

Like the artist in his studio, the person in a life must create from the inside out rather than relying on some great blueprint in the sky to justify her actions here on earth. But if one never gets very far from the "inside" of the present moment, then the pursuit of pleasure remains at the mercy of animal instincts and immediate impulses. The pursuit of pleasure in the immediate moment can be cultivated by widening the horizon of anticipation. The pursuit of pleasure can gain the sophistication of a philosophy: hedonism.

2. HEDONISM

Pleasure is a great teacher when it comes to the folly of instrumental rationality, the belief that *all* activity is a means toward an end. Who among us has not experienced the anguish of failed hedonism? You think you know just what it will take to make you feel wonderful. You get all the means and instruments just right—the setting, the music, the companion, the clothes—and somehow the very accuracy of the contrivance confounds the delight that was expected. Pleasure is tricky that way. It relies on the unexpected. Like art and humor, it eludes explanation and defies careful planning. You cannot make pleasure your *goal* or you will lessen the likelihood of its unexpected eruption. Pleasure can be courted but not calculated.

3. CYNICISM

Cynics are entirely too calculating, too quick to see the vanity of all things and the worthlessness of any and every candidate for delight. Theirs is a sourness that has seen it all, a worldly "wisdom" that renders the soul incapable of spontaneity.

Cynicism is tempting to intellectuals who pride themselves on their ability to *see through appearances*. The greatest sin for an intellectual is naiveté—taking things at face value. So there is a tendency to look for depth even where there is none. Among intellectuals there is a natural tendency to slip into emotional as well as intellectual depths. The depression that often comes with cynicism has a certain intellectual respectability: at least one hasn't taken any wooden nickels or fallen for any false goals. There is a cognitive comfort that depression provides: for once one knows something with certainty. One *knows* that nothing is worthwhile. The corrosive power of cynicism eats through all goals, leaving the cynic no source of enthusiasm.

4. BUDDHISM

Like the cynic, the Buddhist practices nonattachment or desirelessness. Like the cynic, the Buddhist seeks liberation from the hedonist's attachment to desire's goal: immediate pleasure. But there is a difference between Buddhism and cynicism, a difference that is not always easy to discern. The Buddhist lives in a way that is beyond the calculation of relative grades of disappointment. Nirvana is a kind of oriental beatitude that comes with the emptying of the mind, not as the result of mental calculation.

The Buddhist notion of nonattachment captures something of the idea of Goallessness. At first glance nonattachment looks like an oath of poverty: you give up your attachments to *things*. But just as important is surrendering attachment to specific *outcomes* of your actions—goals. This active-passive state of being is not necessarily a state of doing nothing. Zen texts speak of a doing that is a nondoing. There is a certain quality of concentration in which the doer disappears and the doing is everything. Buddhists call it no-mind, a contemplative state of being that allows the lotus blossom to contemplate the contemplator. Heidegger called it *Gelassenheit*, a letting-be-what-is. Nietzsche was also well aware of this kind of *doing*. In *The Genealogy of Morals*, he writes, "There is no 'being' behind the doing, acting, becoming; the 'doer' has simply been added to the deed by the imagination—the doing is everything."

5. SLOTH

We know about doing nothing, an insidious form of goalless-ness, the slough of unresponsiveness to every invitation to action. Not this, not that. Nothing seizes and holds one's interest. Nothing seems worth the effort. But it is not enough just to *be*. It is not enough for those of us who are obsessive doers simply to exist in the avoidance of pain or hunger. The state of satisfaction is necessarily short-lived because you worry: *Am I accomplishing enough? Have I earned the air I breathe? Am I being lazy?*

And what if the answer is yes? What if you allow yourself to loaf? What then? Must there be guilt? Must there be a self-excoriation? Yes, sometimes there must. This discourse on Goallessness is not designed to let us off all hooks. When you have made a promise to yourself or to someone else, and that promise requires of you that you do some work, then it is wrong to put aside that work in the name of Goallessness and just sitting.

You may think that history has promised something to you, that you have some particular destiny that will pull you along without much effort. But beware destiny's reductionism. Look out for the way concentration on a particular destiny reduces the present to the lowly status of a paving stone toward a predestined future.

No goal can be so demanding that it compromises our sense of who it is who is achieving that goal. This is always the risk, isn't it? That a goal will lift us out of our laziness and demand so much of us that the reward will be enjoyed by someone quite other than the self who set out to achieve it. This is why we fear obsessions, even though our obsessions are such good substitutes for goals.

6. OBSESSION

Obsessions can serve as a substitute for goals by giving a direction to life. Where destiny provides a direction by pulling us toward a particular future, the pressure of obsession is more like a push from a past we cannot shake.

Obsession is actually a kind of blessing, though it is usually thought of as a curse. Obsession brooks no doubts about the object of desire. Obsession is not subject to doubt. None of this "to be or not to be" stuff. None of this *Could I be mistaken?* with obsession.

The intensity of obsession might seem to have the constricting squeeze of a goal. But our obsessions drive us to excitement without confining us to a single path. The intense focus of obsession finds fine-grained details that are infinite in their variety. To the fisherman obsessed, no two fishing trips are the same. Pity the casual fisherman, for he will get bored with the waiting. No two golf games are the same for the obsessive golfer. Pity the casual golfer, for he will never reduce his handicap. Likewise, no two ski runs are the same. Pity the casual skier, for she will never dance off the tops of moguls. And no two seductions are the same. Pity casual lovers, for they will not know passion.

Some obsessions are not harmless, and they are the ones that should be sacrificed on the altar of Goallessness: the obsession with wealth that turns into insatiable greed, or the obsession with sex that reduces all of life to an endless chase. But beware of all that is casual: casual dress, casual evenings, casual affronts. They hide a diffidence that runs deeper than the contrived superficiality of the casual pose.

7. THE END OF HISTORY AND THE GOAL OF PROGRESS

Francis Fukuyama brilliantly but misleadingly announced "the end of history," a prospect that would seem to remove the Goal of progress. Fukuyama takes the demise of Marxism as the definitive sign of the end of the ideological, right/left, political struggle. Further, "the death of this ideology means the growing 'Common Marketization' of international relations, and the diminution of the likelihood of large-scale conflict between states."

Is peace on earth the prelude to utopia? Not quite. "The end of history will be a very sad time," writes Fukuyama. "The struggle for recognition, *the willingness to risk one's life for a purely abstract goal,* the worldwide ideological struggle that called for daring, courage, imagination, and idealism, will be replaced by economic calculation, the endless solving of technical problems, environmental concerns, and the satisfaction of sophisticated consumer demands. In the post-historical period there will be neither art nor philosophy, just the perpetual caretaking of the museum of human history . . . centuries of boredom. . . ."

Though I agree with Fukuyama's appreciation for the move from a political to an economic logic of history, I part company with him when he reaches his "centuries of boredom" without art or philosophy. Art and philosophy pick up precisely where the lockstep of political history leaves off. Only *after* the boring pendulum swings of political history have ceased their repetitive cycles from right to left, left to right, right to left, can we get on with the less mechanical creativity of art and philosophy.

Only now can we put the mechanics of the political/industrial modern era behind us, transcend the realm of necessity, enter into the realm of freedom, and begin making up life as we go along as artistically as possible. Only now can we be liberated from the political and industrial goals that turn us into *functionaries* so that we can finally become *artists* of human life.

Will there be any passion in a life devoid of transcendent purposes like religious crusades or revolutionary fervors? Must we have banners to march under, ideologies to light our paths? Once all the Grand Goals have been deconstructed, are we condemned to boredom, or can we find a lyricism in the little things in life? Is it small-minded to scale back the scope of human concerns from the cosmic to the historical to the everyday? I don't think so, for the immensity of each moment, seen from a perspective that is unconstrained by the literalism of physical dimensions, is sometimes more than one can bear. Living without a Goal calls for sources of meaning that don't rely on literal immensity.

At the end of any era there is likely to be a great deal of lamentation, gnashing of teeth and talk of the death of this and the death of that. We are now passing through such a period in history. Hence the great unhappiness of people who were living in tune with the institutional structures that are now crumbling. Individuals are not immune to influences from their institutional environments. The family, the shape of work, the fabric of relationships that make up a life, are all subject to historical change. And when one historical epoch gives way to another, a personality built for one era can feel painfully disjointed when it finds itself in the next, like a person who packed for the wrong trip.

HOW DID WE pack for this trip? How did we fall for slavery to Grand Goals? Simply, really. You can hear the typical speeches that hold him or her in chains: "If I quit this job, will I find another as good? I need this job to pay for the car, the apartment. Maybe this job will lead to a better, higher-paying job, and a better car, and a house . . ."

And then what? Over the horizon of the present, a "better" future beckons. A "better" job. A "better" home. So the present becomes a brief indignity best forgotten. The present becomes tedious, a time of preparing. You grow impatient with the pace of this present. You resolve to work harder, to hasten the arrival of your future Goal.

Your freedom could be enhanced by some embellishments on the bare necessities: better clothes, a bigger home, more free time. But these improvements require resources. You notice that the people with resources have jobs with fancier titles and bigger salaries. In order to get one of those jobs, to get the resources, to improve your life, you must prepare for the kind of career that offers a bigger paycheck. So you go to school, which you see as a preparation for life, not life itself. You do your homework. You become used to existing in a present that is a pale anticipation of a better future. You become used to striving toward a distant Goal. School then prepares you to live in a way that is not really living but a perpetual preparation for life.

Let's say you are not expelled for any transgressions; you accomplish the goal of graduation. By now the direction of your education is no longer *your* goal, strictly speaking, but a series of goals set by your teachers: a curriculum. But you dutifully jump through all the hoops and over bars whose heights your teachers keep raising. You may take little delight in these gymnastics, whether literal or intellectual, because after all they are only a preparation for The Real Thing. But let's say you succeed in covering all of the courses in the preparatory curriculum, and you are ready to graduate. You have accomplished your goal. But have you? For in the course of your studies new horizons have been opened to you. There are schools beyond the school you just finished, schools with longer curricula leading toward careers that are much more alluring than the sort of job you first had in mind. So you show that you have learned your lessons well by doing for yourself what your teachers had earlier done for you: *you raise the bar yourself.* You set yourself a higher Goal.

The story thus far may be vague in its outlines but familiar in its plot. You can fill in precise details with the name of your school, the date of your graduation. But then things probably get fuzzy, as they tend to do in that further curriculum, the one whose goal is neither Mother Nature's necessities nor the goals set by others. Chances are you think you are supposed to have a precise Goal for life's curriculum, but you don't really, so you are slightly guilty that you can't articulate very precisely the Goal you think you are supposed to have. This ill-defined Goal has both the nobility and the mysteriousness of God. This hazy objective, surrounded by clouds like the peak of Mount Olympus, commands your reverence. This elusive Goal also reduces your adulthood to childish subservience.

The moral of this story is clear: beware of enslaving yourself to some single overriding Goal. Your freedom may get overridden. But if you abandon all goals, you risk sliding into abject aimlessness. Not only does your life lack a meaning; so does the next moment. Why get out of bed in the morning? This book is therefore devoted to finding the zone between meaninglessness and Meaning. How do you give meaning to your days without having found The Meaning of Life?

The next chapter outlines the zone between Meaning and meaninglessness by personifying its outer boundaries. We will meet Lila, a Goal junkie who depends on Meaning, and Spike, a guy who gets tattooed because, hell, why not? Subsequent chapters will speak first to Lila, to follow her journey from one Grand Goal to another; and then to Spike, to lure him out of his narcissistic retreat into the pit of nihilistic goallessness (note the little *g*). By the time the third movement begins, Spike and Lila's lives will have converged toward a love that is more committed and goal-laden than Spike's impulses of the moment, yet less fraught with Meaning than the Perfect Love that Lila seeks as a Goal. By tacking back and forth between extremes that may at first appeaer as cartoon stereotypes, the rest of the book will fill in that zone between Meaning and meaninglessness, between the pursuit of Grand Goals and an aimless nihilism.

Two Extremes: Lila and Spike

MAN WOULD SOONER HAVE THE VOID FOR HIS
PURPOSE THAN BE VOID OF PURPOSE.

—*Nietzsche*

2

IVING WITHOUT A GOAL OCCU-
pies a zone that is fuzzily bounded on
one side by abject goallessness and on the
other by life in pursuit of a Grand Goal.
Because the boundaries are fuzzy, best to mark them with concrete and complicated lives rather than misleadingly elegant
theories. Lila lives most of her life in quest of a Grand Goal—
including at one point the void. Spike is attempting to be void
of purpose. By getting acquainted with Spike and Lila, we will
become more familiar with the zone of Goallessness between
them.

Lila is a woman of forty-five living in Los Angeles, or
perhaps Eugene. She's lived most of her life in thrall to one
Grand Goal or another, but now she's confused. She's just

walked away from the third job she's started since her divorce. Life hasn't worked out quite the way Lila expected.

Lila is not particularly hard up. She got a terrific settlement from a car accident six years ago. A Postal Service truck lost its brakes and creamed her Volvo station wagon. And her second husband, the one who bought the Volvo, is still making alimony payments. But work gives her something to do. If she weren't working, she'd be spending more time on Dr. Wasserstein's couch worrying about the meter ticking over at two-fifty a minute. When she's not working, she gets depressed and then grasps at straws, struggling to get back on track.

There have been a lot of different tracks, all of them eventually leading nowhere. And now she's beginning to wonder whether she'll ever find the path, the way, the Tao. . . . So many trips! She was seventeen when she graduated from high school in 1967, headed west in June and reached Haight Ashbury just in time for the "Summer of Love." She was so hopeful then, so full of love. But by September all she had to show for it were hazy memories of a string of bearded faces and a wardrobe of flowing tie-dyed frocks.

That winter she became more discerning. She had this yen to save the world, and she needed help. She started looking for Her Man. She met Russ at an SDS meeting. He spoke with such passion, shaking his long dark hair out of his eyes as he laid down his political analyses. Russ introduced Lila to injustice. She hadn't really thought about it all that much, but when she watched the muscles in his unshaven jaw clench with anger, she became completely convinced that her Goal in life was to topple the oppressors: racists, warmongers, fat cats. Only later did the list include *men*.

For the better part of five years—from '68 until 1973—she

was dedicated to The Movement. So many meetings, so many sit-ins, so many marches. She kept up with her studies at S. F. State—when she wasn't shutting it down. She took courses in philosophy and political science. Senior year she wrote a long paper on the Italian Marxist Antonio Gramsci—something just relevant enough to keep her in school, and esoteric enough to give her real clout when arguing late at night with the Stalinists who were taking over SDS. Even Russ was impressed.

Then Watergate broke, the Vietnam War ended, and nobody came to the meetings anymore. The whole political thing just fizzled. The preferred way to stay with it was to go even further left, dive down into the Weather underground and learn how to make bombs. Too much! Lila just wasn't that *sure*. She fled when Russ started mixing Molotov cocktails in the commune's kitchen.

LOTUS BLOSSOM RANCH, a commune organized around more peaceable principles, was located about ten miles outside of Taos. That's where Lila met Philip, a wispy young man committed to Tibetan Buddhism, yoga and organic gardening—much better hobbies than fanatic macrobiotics and Molotov cocktails. Lila got into the gardening. And even though she had at first criticized some of the communards for slipping into bourgeois subjectivism, eventually she got into the meditating too. It felt so good when the whole commune sat silently in a circle. Sometimes they held hands. Sometimes they broke silence and filled the meditation yurt with the most amazing Oms you've ever heard. Philip was particularly adept at making overtones up in his sinuses. He really got her kundalini going.

Her problem with Buddhism was no longer the tendency toward bourgeois subjectivism. Now her problem was the doctrine of desirelessness. She desired Philip a lot. Their guru—an aging Roshi who visited the ranch a couple of times a year—went so far as to accuse Lila of Tantric heresy during one of their week-long sasheens. She worked on it. She tried to overcome her desires. She tried to ignore her desires. She tried to sublimate her desires through redoubled efforts in the garden. Then she got pregnant.

Michael Ashanti Bowman was born in the middle of a blizzard during the cold winter of 1975. Bowman was Philip's last name. Ashanti came from the guru. Michael was the name of Lila's favorite grandfather. After a long bout with cancer, old Michael died almost the moment young Michael was conceived. Lila liked to believe that the elder Michael's soul migrated straight from his dying body into the new life in her womb.

Lila loved taking care of the baby. For the first time in her life she felt absolutely certain about her Goal. She hadn't been sure enough about the revolution to mix cocktails. She had never been completely committed to the goal of spiritual enlightenment if that meant surrendering her desires. But now the goal of raising a perfect being descended upon her. She was suddenly completely sure. There were no debates over correct analyses, no paradoxical koans to unravel in the depths of meditation, just a calm certainty she felt when his warm baby mouth suckled at her breast. Finally Lila began to taste the sweet fruit of happiness. At last she knew what her life was about: motherhood. What a crashing disappointment it therefore was when she discovered feminism.

While taking care of Mikey she picked her way through

some books left behind by an old friend from S. F. State. Simone de Beauvoir's *Second Sex* appealed to her philosophy major's taste. She had studied Sartre's late Marxist writings in the course of her research on Gramsci, and any friend of Jean Paul Sartre's would be a friend of hers. But de Beauvoir, Sartre's lifelong lover, was no friend of conventional motherhood. Nefariously planted in Lila's bedroom by her still political friend from the Haight, de Beauvoir's book erupted like a time bomb, obliterating Lila's calm certainty about motherhood as the be-all and end-all of her existence. How had she been so blind? How had she been so deluded about her goal in life? Hadn't she learned about false consciousness from her reading of Marx and Gramsci? But it took Simone de Beauvoir to put it all into the perspective of the battle between the sexes.

Lila started getting on Philip about washing the dishes. Then it was the diapers. Before long there was a campaign to split the housework fifty-fifty. After all, didn't she do her share of heavy lifting in the garden—all those loads of mulch, and bringing in the harvest? But if Philip was going to split the housework, that meant splitting the parenting as well. Once Mikey was weaned, there was hardly anything Lila did that Philip couldn't do as well. But did he? Of course not. So Lila moved by reluctant fits and starts ever closer to militancy. And further from total devotion to motherhood. And further from Philip.

CHRISTMAS, 1978, SHE went home for the holidays to visit her mother and grandmother in Columbus, Ohio. Grandma had moved in with Mom after Michael died. The three women—twenty-eight, sixty, and eighty-eight—fitted well together. Lila was surprised. But she was getting old enough to forgive her parents for making a mess of things.

With Grampa Michael and her father gone, the three generations of Thompson women fell into a new solidarity with one another. Finally Lila had real help with parenting. She never went back to Taos. She filed for divorce in Columbus and Philip traded custody for no alimony. He never had any money anyway.

Money was a problem for the three women. Michael didn't leave much, and neither did Lila's father. Just a paid-off mortgage and a closet full of clothes that he hardly needed for his new life as a sport fisherman. After a life as a Midwestern housewife, Lila's mother was short on marketable skills. So it quickly fell to Lila to pay for groceries, uninsured medical bills for Grandma and upkeep on the aging house.

With the benefit of built-in baby-sitters, Lila took a full-time job at the bank her father had left. Uncle Paul, her father's former partner, felt badly about the way his former friend had ditched the family. He wanted to help out. Despite her lack of skills, he convinced Lila to sign up for the bank's teller training program.

Going back to school wasn't as bad as Lila expected it to be. It was mostly on-the-job training—a lot of doing, not so much talking and writing. She was on her feet more than in a chair, face to face more than alone, and she liked it. She liked solving soluble problems, even though they were little ones. She liked reconciling her accounts at the end of each day. It was satisfying in a way that unending jobs never were. Neither the revolution nor enlightenment ever quite arrived, ~~and mothering arrived so reliably again and again~~ that it was never done. But her teller's books opened and closed each and every day with the satisfying certainty of a safe door closing shut.

LILA LIKED HER new job at first. But a teller's life is tedious once you know how to do it. And being in the immediate presence of all that money, but taking home so little of it, Lila got to thinking. There must be an easier way. . . . Her thoughts did not drift to larceny. Her sense of justice forbade theft. But she wasn't against applying a little ingenuity to increase her yield. The question was, how?

In 1980 she entered the MBA program at Northwestern. Sure she had ambivalences. She hadn't forgotten all those late nights of radical analysis. But times had changed and she had changed and Mikey needed clothes and karate lessons and much, much more.

Once she got to it, Lila was amazed at how little of her past she had to forget. There was a lot about Gramsci's notion of praxis that applied to entrepreneurship—the importance of action and experimentation, the need to modify theory in the light of practice rather than forcing new practice to conform to old theory. And marketing, particularly promotions, wasn't that different from community organizing. Sales is sales, she concluded, whether you're selling revolution or soap. Some of the brightest of her fellow students, she eventually discovered, had been active in The Movement. Did they share the guilty secret of betraying youthful commitments? Or had they refocused their commitment? They didn't talk about it much. Nor did they hide their pasts. Lila joined her classmates on a journey that had many stops. She was no longer as sure about just where the journey was going.

At Northwestern she met Kim, an ex-rad who believed in making the system work for us instead of against us. There was nothing wispy about Kim. He was strong and motivated—a bundle of loose energy looking for a task. Kim and Lila started running together in the early mornings. By second year they were living together. When they both got jobs as investment analysts with Chase Manhattan in Chicago, that seemed adequate grounds for tying the knot.

Life wasn't simple. Lila spent weekends in Columbus with Mikey and the mothers, weeks in Chicago with Kim and Chase. But it seemed to work. And work and work. She worked very hard, but there were rewards: cash, achievement, new friends, a sense of excitement. She and Kim saw one another passing in the halls at Chase, but often didn't get home till after ten, exhausted. The morning run gave way to morning love. Life was good. Life was rich. By 1987 they were able to get a place big enough for Mikey and one more. The baby room was ready for Tracey when she came home from the hospital on Easter morning, 1988. Mikey told his friends about what the Easter Bunny brought to his house.

Kim was carving out a niche in financing in the entertainment industry. He wasn't just good at the mathematics. He was good at doing deals. In 1989 he got an offer to join a talent agency in Hollywood. They moved. Once in Tinseltown, however, Kim's loose energy got looser. He couldn't handle the updraft. The cocaine and the babes got to him. In 1991 he walked out on Lila and the kids.

TO QUOTE A song that Lila's been playing a lot lately—now on CD with none of the old scratches and pops—"What a long strange trip it's been—Truckin'." Now forty-five, reasonably well financed, educated, two kids, fairly accomplished . . . what next? And why? Can she find a new Goal to get her out of bed in the morning? Does she need one?

I say, no! She doesn't need some grand shining Goal to light her path into her future. She's just starting to learn how to make it up as she goes along, and that's more like life than laying down her soul in the service of some grand and shining purpose like revolution or enlightenment or, for that matter, Kim.

SPIKE

Spike's another story. He needs goals. Not a Goal, but goals, because right now he's got none. Nada. No future whatever, and he's proud of it.

Spike grew up on Sid Vicious and the Sex Pistols. It's not that Spike is vicious or evil. But his stated opinions about the future run toward the morbid. He's just twenty-six, and part of the back end of the baby boom for whom all the goodies are preassigned. He's given to saying things like, "Demography is destiny, and ours sucks. What have I got to look forward to? I'm an aspiring dead white male."

Spike is resigned to a life entirely out of his own control. He hears about oil prices and the impact of oscillations in the yen/dollar exchange rate. He knows he has about as much chance of changing these conditioners of his life as he has influence over the cycle of sunspots.

Global warming? Cool. Better to blow out a single match than curse the heat.

Spike prefers cartoons to the news. Watching cartoons tells him more about what's really going on in his head. You think adult cartoons are cute? You think Rocky and Bullwinkle and the Simpsons and Ren and Stimpy promise fun for the whole family with their layered meanings and generation-spanning double entendres? But what about the kids? What's it like to learn to laugh *knowing* that you don't get the whole joke?

What does little Spike learn when Bart Simpson's little sister gets *bad?* When a callow adult asks her, "But what are you rebelling against?" and she answers, "Whaddaya got?"

If most of your vivid experience has been mediated by the media, you gain a taste for immediacy: raw footage, unanalyzed, no color commentary, no spin. But the media won't play it raw. The media insist on mediating: censorship for family viewing, and a spin on the news to add interpretation and meaning. The downside of raw experience is that it's meaningless. Take away the mediation and you take away the meaning. So take your pick: meaninglessness or the mediation of the spin doctors.

Spike and his friends pick both. Who cares about consistency? They indulge a taste for raw experience. They worship the holy trinity: sex, drugs and rock'n'roll. But they play at meaningful moments. They like sending each other Hallmark cards with prepackaged, heartfelt messages nestled among lilacs and irises.

Irony is fun but, to Spike and his friends, cynics are boring. Cynicism is so predictable. In his heart of hearts Spike knows that he dismisses all cant and hypocrisy because somewhere, somehow, he got a taste of what it feels like to be authentic. He just can't remember exactly where or how.

Virtue is real for Spike, but it exists only on another planet, or in places with names like Gdansk and Prague among people with names like Lech or Vaclev. He sees few opportunities for virtue at the mall.

Spike knows there's something better than life at the mall, but he's lost his map. He can't find the way out. He can't even find the red dot that says, "You are here."

THE GREAT THING about drugs is that they break the boredom. Talk about switching the channel! Talk about Technicolor! We're talking neon dreams. But the body suffers. So Spike works hard to maintain his temple of doom. He needs to buttress his biceps and care for those quads. He takes vitamins. He stays away from steroids. His body is the closest thing he will ever know to a safe environment.

His horror of AIDS is not that some humongous germ will invade the fortress of his body. His horror of autoimmune deficiency is the prospect of his own private army of guardians simply laying down their arms so that any puny illness—a common cold—can wipe him out. It is the horror of defense-lessness. A body needs *more* than the usual defenses these days, not less.

Bodies are real. Unlike a series of McJobs leading nowhere, bodies are cumulative. Bodies have memories, and maybe even futures. Be kind to your body, says Spike. It is, perhaps, your most faithful friend. It will not betray you, at least not until it gets old. Nurture your body. Beware of filling it with the flesh of dead animals. Eat fiber. Work out. So Spike is into body building. There's something so immediate about pumping iron. It's like a red dot. You know you're here. You can forget about *there,* and the fact that you don't have a map to get you from here to there.

Whenever Spike has doubts about his place in the cosmos, which happens fairly often, he can always exercise in front of a mirror. Look at those stomach muscles! See those swelling pecs! And *feel* the effort. For once there's a clear and evident connection between what he feels inside and sees outside.

Spike fell in love with his image in the gym mirror long before he discovered that narcissism was a sin. His guiltless infatuation with his own rippling muscles wasn't anything he felt bad about until he saw a bunch of body builders get torn apart one afternoon on "Oprah." The moms of America clearly liked the rippling muscles. But they didn't like the way the guys liked their own rippling muscles. A couple of moms started talking about narcissism and Spike learned a new word. He looked it up in the dictionary: "*n.* in psychoanalysis, an abnormal love and admiration for oneself."

Spike felt a twinge of recognition. "Uh-oh. 'In *psychoanalysis,*' huh?" Pretty soon he started to pick up on other references to the dread disease. One night he met a lovely young lady at a party, got her to come back to his loft and enjoyed the delights of true lust with her only to have her comment when she came up for air, "Look at all those mirrors. You must be some kind of narcissist!" That was all she had to say. Suddenly his mirrors weren't as much fun anymore. What happens when impotence strikes at the heart of the romance of self-love?

LOVE ? SPIKE'S PARENTS inspire neither envy nor emulation. Spike feels the urge. The plumbing works. His hormones are in order. But the songs he remembers from his formative years have titles like, "Love Hurts," and "Total Eclipse of the Heart."

Like virtue, Spike suspects, love is real for creatures on some other planet. For himself, he's gotten really good at masturbation. Spike thinks he's immune to loneliness. There will always be television, with even more channels to come, and some of them, they say, *interactive.* Virtual love is, like, real enough for Spike.

Fame? Spike suspects he'll get his fifteen minutes sooner or later. Maybe he'll be lucky enough to get interviewed at the scene of a disaster.

Friends? Oh yes. Friendship is very real. When families are a joke, when work sucks, when love hurts, then friendship counts. Spike and his friends are friends for life. But life is, like, short.

(Older people don't like the way Spike and his friends pepper their speech with the word "like." Why do they do it? Ask them and they'll say, "It's, like, you know . . ." And we who still have vocabularies *should* know: that nothing in their world simply *is* what it is. Everything now is *like* something else. Language cannot simply name or describe anymore. With reality gone surreal, language can only sneak up on things obliquely. If the surrealist André Breton is right that "existence is *elsewhere*," then all the kids can do *here* is talk about what things are *like*.)

LIKE SO MANY cordless phones, reality has come untethered. Given a multiple choice quiz on the meaning of the word "anchor," the kids will pass over "mooring for a boat" and check "biggest store in the mall." And if Wittgenstein is correct in telling us that the meaning of a word is its *use*, then of course they are right and we are wrong to lower their SAT scores. Are the kids dumb and ignorant about *The* world, or are the test makers ignorant of the test takers' world?

Spike knows the meanings of words that are foreign language to his parental units, words like "kevlar" and "tunage." His vocabulary is filled with hyphens unknown to earlier generations: "hard-drive," "value-added," "fast-forward."

Is there any wonder Spike is blind to Old World goals? Sure, he wants to be rich. Poverty sucks, and it's not the least bit cool either. But Spike knows better than to imagine that a college degree and hard work will win the sweepstakes. No hoops and high bars for Spike. He knows that a sense of humor and the right friends will get him a lot further than whatever he can learn in school.

SPIKE MAY NOT get lonely, but he does get horny. His animal parts erupt from time to time and drive him well-nigh crazy with desire. So he goes to the beach and trolls for flesh, preferably the kind that doesn't know words like "narcissistic." His tastes have been running to teens of late, and his friends are getting on him for it.

"Taut, yes, but undeserved. What we achieve with sweat is theirs merely by virtue of their callow youth," says Spike's unusually articulate friend Alan, appraising Spike's latest. "Cindy clearly adores you. And her mom's BMW *does* have great sound. But, Spike, m'man, will the conversation last through, like, dessert? I mean . . ."

Spike is protective: of Cindy? Or of his own taste? He's not just sure. But Alan's challenge makes him more tender toward Cindy than he might otherwise have been. "She's . . . sweet," is all he says, and therefore sees her so.

That night he actually feels pangs of morality before he finally deflowers her. Remarkable. Who would've guessed that, at eighteen . . . She should've *told* him instead of letting blood speak. Why, after all, did the good Lord invent words? He actually had to *ask* her whether it was her period, and she actually had to explain. Reality is so surreal, even when it's actual.

The real, the surreal, the actual—do philosophers have room in their somber ontologies for these subtle gradations? Spike doesn't use words like "ontology," the logos or science of Being. But he can spot a fake Rolex across a firm handshake. Spike has a keen eye for all that is phony. In that sense, he is an inverse connoisseur of grades of Being, whether or not he knows anything about ontology.

"What do we do now?" she asked. "Get married?" And for three nanoseconds of tenderness, Spike's first feeling was yes. But he got the better of himself and laughed. So, of course, she cried.

"What we do is we go on just as before. You are too young to get married. I may want you, but I don't have a clue about what I want to do with my life, and, frankly, I don't even want to think about it. So back off with the marriage talk. Here, let me dry your eyes," he said as he dabbed at her cheek with his Pearl Jam T-shirt.

"But I've been saving it for . . ."

"Jeezus, what planet are you from? What century? Are you trying to guilt-trip me into marriage just because you chose to string out the virgin thing until now?"

More tears. Major waterworks.

"Sorry. Jeez. I guess I'm a real prick," and he set about there-thereing her into cuddled submission. Comforting her tired him, like a parent falling asleep while putting a child to bed. Spike finds responsibility *so* exhausting.

Sometimes Spike suffers a lethargy so heavy as to crush every effort at achievement. A refusal to work wells up from the soles of his feet like a wildcat strike of every neuron in his nervous system. The couch sends out a magnetic field that pulls him toward its cushions. The bed cries out for company. It is not sleep that beckons but inaction, a torpor so deep that nothing short of a fire alarm could raise him.

Sometimes there are specific tasks, sometimes very small ones that keep him from accomplishing anything else for hours. Like tiny mice holding an elephant at bay, they lay themselves before his path and prevent him from doing anything else.

SPIKE AND LILA live just outside opposite boundaries of artful Goallessness. Lila lives much of her life in quest of a Goal: first social justice, then spiritual enlightenment, then love and motherhood, then money. Without one of these massive Goals, she doesn't know how to get through her days. She desperately needs a map and a destination. Without a map, she gets depressed and lands on Dr. Wasserstein's couch.

Spike is mapless, but also artless. Singed by hopelessness, he has retreated into a narcissistic grotto of self without other, present without future, here without there. If Lila needs to contract her horizons from noble destinations that are *there*, Spike needs to expand his horizons beyond the red dot marking *here*.

But how to get Spike beyond *here* without selling him some bogus story about a Goal he would never buy? And how to convince Lila that she doesn't need a Grand Goal to light her path to *there?*

TRADING GOALS

It is only late that one musters the courage for what one really knows. . . . When one moves toward a goal it seems impossible that "goallessness as such" is the principle of our faith.

—*Nietzsche*

3

OR A FEW BRIGHT SHINING MO-
ments in the late sixties, it seemed the
goal of freedom could be achieved with a
singular, once-and-for-all liberation from
the repressive weight of tradition. One more march on Wash-
ington, wished Lila and her comrades, and peace would be at
hand. One more demonstration and the scales would fall from
the eyes of middle America. Something we called The Transformation would take place and we would all dance hand in
hand to the Grateful Dead. But the revolution didn't happen.
Nineteen sixty-eight in Paris was not like 1917. Political power
did not change hands. Instead, The Transformation changed a
few—but not very many—hearts and minds.

In this chapter I want to review the succession of goals that have obsessed many of my contemporaries over the past few decades. Like Lila, many of us moved through the political passions of the sixties to the spiritual devotions of the seventies and the financial aspirations of the eighties. Annual surveys of college freshmen showed a dramatic shift from 84% coming to college "to gain a meaningful life philosophy" in 1967 down to just 44% with that goal two decades later. Meanwhile the percentage who aspired "to become very well off financially" rose from 44% in 1967 to 75% by 1990.

We had good reasons for pursuing these goals, some of which were admirable. But we didn't always notice the way *we substituted one goal for another to give meaning to our lives*—and that it was *meaning*, the sense of purpose, that was more important than the goals themselves. Nor did we always notice—at least I didn't always notice—how the shape of existence changed as we shifted our attention from one goal to another. Our inventory of the contents of the universe, our sense of what counted, *changed* as we substituted one goal for another. So, after reviewing the succession of goals we've grasped to give meaning to our lives, I'll dig down beneath the succession of job descriptions to show the difference between what counted *then* and what counts *now*.

I REMEMBER HUDDLING under my desk during the air-raid drills of the fifties, but the threat didn't feel real until the Russians grabbed the lead in the space race. When word came down that the Russians had put a satellite into orbit, America shuddered. Sputnik struck fear into the hearts of parents across the land. Suddenly America had a goal: beat the Russkies. Put a man on the moon by the end of the sixties.

The purpose of the Apollo Project beckoned with admirable precision—like its namesake, the Greek god of clarity and light and unambiguous boundaries. A man on the moon was the goal, and science and technology the means. As a student in the fifties and early sixties, my life had a shining purpose, and the means to fulfill that purpose seemed obvious.

Inspired by the goal of winning the space race, and the sense that science and technology could provide the tools for achieving every goal, I decided as a student to major in math and physics. Despite my expulsion from Exeter, I was accepted at Williams, aided perhaps by the fact that my father and uncle had attended. There I learned Schrödinger's wave equation, a single equation that describes the energies of every single particle in the universe. Schrödinger's wave equation seemed to hold the key to the universe. It served as the Goal of my studies in physics, the Holy Grail of my quest. I thought that, once I understood Schrödinger's wave equation, all the mysteries of the universe would be revealed. A new lucidity would leave no doubts about the fundamental nature of reality. After all, if everything is made of atoms, and one understands the law that governs the behavior of atoms, then one would have the key to everything. Right?

Wrong. I had not yet read Irving Copi's *Introduction to Logic* and did not appreciate the "Fallacy of Composition." Just because every little thing in your luggage is light, it does not follow that your luggage is light. Nor if your luggage is heavy does it follow that everything in your luggage is heavy.

You could look at my mistake as a failure to understand the

importance of the rules under which a law can be legitimately applied, what scientists call its *boundary conditions.* Just because all the players and the ball are subject to the law of gravity, you can't logically deduce the rules of baseball from the law of gravity. On my quest to master the most widely applicable, most general laws governing the motion of matter in space and time, I neglected the importance of specifics. I ignored the particular boundary conditions under which Schrödinger's wave equation or Newton's laws might be applied in particular situations.

So it came as a shock to me that, even after I had mastered Schrödinger's wave equation, I still had problems with my love life! I didn't understand that my newfound ability to predict the position of a subatomic particle counted for nothing when it came to predicting the behavior of students at Bennington College just up the road in Vermont. I would have gotten closer to my romantic goal with a bouquet of flowers. But I was blind to the utility of such apparently useless blossoms.

I fell for a knee-jerk physicalism and materialism in my pursuit of mastery over my teenage environment, as if life were one very large game of billiards, its challenge one of figuring out "the angles," and action a matter of getting the right force and direction on my cue stick. As a student in the fifties and early sixties, I found it entirely reasonable to set the precise mastery of matter as my goal. But metal bending and mass production are now yielding to information processing and services as the principal means of adding value in the postindustrial economy. And information processing doesn't follow a tool-and-die logic of forces and impacts, or weights and shapes. The digital dance of 1s and 0s takes place in the ethereal realm of Boolean algebra, not the physical realm of substances, causes and effects.

AS MY GENERALIZED disappointment with Schrödinger's wave equation settled in, I gradually came to understand that I hadn't really been pursuing *physics* in the first place. I'd been pursuing *metaphysics*. In my godless belief in materialism, I was convinced that an understanding of the physical laws governing the movement of matter in space and time was the proper means toward the Goal of mastering the ultimate truths of the universe.

I was neither the first nor the last to look to physics for answers about how to be a human being. The whole tradition of materialists holds the belief that, if you understand matter, in some sense or other you will understand everything. But in what sense? This is a question of philosophy. Philosophy of science, perhaps, but philosophy nonetheless.

So I concluded, at the age of eighteen, that I had been pursuing the *wrong goal*. The philosophy of materialism, not the physics of matter, became my preoccupation. At the time I was not thinking about materialism as consumer lust for industrial goods. Nor was I much aware of materialism as the basis for Marxist philosophy. But I knew I wanted to turn the darkness of mystery into the light of soluble problems. I thought it would be possible to reduce all of the inexact sciences down to the precision and exactitude of math and physics. But in order to test whether this reduction to firm foundations was possible, I had to study not just physics and mathematics but philosophy as well.

So it goes. Answer one question and it leads to another. The Goal of ultimate understanding keeps receding ever farther the more one understands the inadequacy of one's understandings. One step forward, two steps back on a physical path that, like the yellow brick road, had to have an end. But as long as I felt the mental security of a physical path between my feet, I was eager to proceed. If philosophy was to be the next step, so be it. I became a philosophy major.

I TRADED THE Goal of mastering matter for the pursuit of wisdom. But where to find wisdom? Philosophy, it turns out, is not as straightforward as some other disciplines. Philosophy makes no progress. We still read Plato and Aristotle. Unlike physics, philosophy is not cumulative. The history of philosophy does not present us with a record of achievements piled one upon another. Instead, wisdom seems just as elusive in our age as in others. But I did not know this when I first set out to master philosophy. So I enrolled in yet another curriculum in the hope that I could pile one course upon another toward the Goal of wisdom.

After college I took a couple of years of graduate courses. Finally I seemed to be on some sort of straight and narrow path toward the relatively high bar of a Ph.D. from Yale. I was particularly eager to understand Hegel better than he could be understood through English translation. I wanted to plunge into the depths of Hegel's system, swallow it whole, hook, line and sinker, rather than picking at it piecemeal like so many American scholars. So I set off for Germany. The choice was significant, for if ever there were a people capable of pursuing a goal, surely it must be the people who embraced "the final solution."

After a few months away from America, I felt myself falling in love with the German people. I liked their healthy good looks and their seriousness of purpose. Americans came to seem frivolous by comparison. And then one day it dawned on me: had I come to Germany in the 1930s with the same goal, I might have been a prime candidate for fascism, ripe for a total and fanatic commitment to the goal of the thousand-year Reich. "The final solution" was the end that would justify any means—a Goal that would supposedly vindicate any horror committed in its name. There I was in the shadow of Heidegger, a very smart philosopher whose Teutonic intensity overcame his sense of human decency to the point that he supported Hitler. If I had come to sit at his feet during the 1930s, my respect and commitment might have led me into the Hitler Youth movement.

This realization shook me to the core. What had seemed to be virtues—hard work, total devotion, delayed gratification—could so easily become vices. What had seemed so unquestionably good—the modest goal of learning German as a means to the end of mastering German philosophy—could have been turned to the service of evil if I had happened into it at the wrong time. This sense of my own fallibility sent me reeling from the relatively safe confines of academic philosophy. I became skeptical about my ability to find life's formula by figuring it out philosophically. Yet I was unable to surrender the Goal of wisdom without sinking into a wretched depression.

I remember days when I left my desk in the library and wandered the streets of Freiburg cursing the sky for its boring blueness. My despair found outlet in hours of pinball. What was the fascination of that game? How could a graduate student with few resources squander so many pfennigs on this foolish game when there was work to be done? Such guilty pleasures. And where was the source of the pleasure? Picking at the wound of my guilt? Or was there a particular appropriateness in my choice of a sin? Wasn't the Newtonian precision of pinball a perfect successor to the billiard table? Pinball provokes a kind of nostalgia for the industrial era. Is this the source of fascination that keeps millions of Japanese in Pachinko parlors? Is the source of the amazing popularity of these Japanese pinball games to be found in a similar nostalgia for physical precision in a confusing world?

Players of pinball see the battle between chance and necessity enacted before their eyes: the inexorable pull of gravity, the precision of those little balls caught in the stochastic dance among pins, the predictable angles caroming off bumpers, the opportunity for human will and skill in exercising a flipper before the ball disappears at the end of the game. Was the psychological satisfaction of these games, all of which come to an end, something akin to Lila's delight in closing her bank teller's books with the finality of a safe door's shutting? All I know is that in my depression I felt some connection between my brush with fascism and my pursuit of a guilty pleasure.

WE DON'T GIVE up our cherished goals lightly. Like Lila, we use our cherished goals as bulwarks against depression. If the present isn't as sweet as we might wish, we can always write off today's pain as a necessary step on the way toward tomorrow's delight. Remove the prospect of tomorrow's reward and today's sacrifice becomes pointless. Today's pain is bearable if it holds some promise of a better tomorrow, if it has some *meaning*, namely, as a sacrifice in the present for the sake of some goal in the future. But once that promise is broken or removed, once the goal of deferred gratification is taken away, then today's pain is pointless . . . and depression sets in. The bearable suffering of an identifiable wound gives way to the unbearable despair that cannot identify its source. The only solace I could find for this loss of an identifiable pain was a philosophy that could provide a text for depression. So I read a lot of Nietzsche and discovered the lines that are the epigram to this chapter: "It is only late that one musters the courage for what one really knows. . . . When one moves toward a goal it seems impossible that 'goallessness as such' is the principle of our faith."

AFTER COMPLETING MY dissertation in Germany, I taught seminars on Nietzsche when I returned to Yale. Once back in the United States, I didn't just teach Nietzsche's goalless nihilism; I lived it . . . almost. I joined what later came to be called a commune. I committed all sorts of foolishness that precluded the tacit goal of gaining academic tenure. Already I had come to suspect that the goals my contemporaries were pursuing were not enough to sustain my life.

Despite my best efforts, I could not maintain the dark demeanor characteristic of the European nihilist. I could dress in black clothing, but I could not maintain a philosophically respectable depression. Beneath my furrowed brow smiles kept breaking through. Was I too shallow for European nihilism?

Perhaps it was the times, the late sixties, heady days when

shaking off our European past seemed not only possible but altogether necessary. Apocalypse was just around the corner. The Living Theater came to New Haven to perform *Apocalypse Now*. They pushed out the boundaries of propriety. They got naked onstage. They shouted about freedom, and suddenly all of the old rules were in jeopardy.

When the Black Panthers came to New Haven to get Bobby Seale out of jail in the spring of 1970, and Nixon sent troops into Cambodia, Yale went on strike. When four students were shot at Kent State, New Haven's mayor called in the National Guard. It occurred to me that there was serious danger of bloodshed within the ivied walls if the radicals insisted on "heightening the contradictions," as they were wont to say and do. I joined the Strike Steering Committee as its only faculty member. I knew I was jeopardizing my chances on the quest for the academic holy grail—the Goal of Tenure. But somehow the moral demands of the moment seemed more pressing than the pull of that remote Goal.

Artists do not expect tenure. Entrepreneurs don't count on the retirement plans offered by large corporations. While civil servants turn gray in their sinecures, the rest of us may be forced to wake up from the sleep that dreams of security. Can we accept the evanescence of events and institutions and learn to navigate without the pole stars of permanent Goals?

BY SUBSTITUTING The Transformation for the bourgeois goals our parents and teachers had set us, the partisans of the New Left did not achieve Nietzsche's goallessness. *We just substituted another goal for those that had been rejected.* The transformation of consciousness, coupled with the transformation of self and the transformation of society, differentiated the goals of the New Left from those of the old left. The goal-directed old left preached the dreary pursuit of revolution, with all its dull economic rhetoric about expropriating the expropriators. The more process-oriented New Left, peopled largely by hippies from the suburbs, said: "Forget all this garbage about *property*. Who wants to mow a bigger lawn? You gotta transform *consciousness!*" Forget the revolution. Social transformation was the Goal, individual transformation the means, so all of that liberating experimentation with sex, drugs and rock'n'roll had a marvelous rationale.

Heady times, the sixties. The colors were very bright. The light kept breaking through. The dark despair of European nihilism just didn't wear well at Woodstock. Nor did a rhetoric of suffering play well in Paris in the spring of 1968. The gospel according to Karl Marx gave way to a heretical turn toward the brothers Groucho, Harpo and Zeppo—politics turned artistic to the point of becoming comic. It wasn't easy to be a nihilist in the late sixties. There was way too much laughter.

Of course *the Goal*—The Transformation—came no closer than the revolution. Flower power was no match for the stolid resistance of middle America. But it sure was fun trying. The Goal of The Transformation kept many of us moving through years of confusion. The Goal of The Transformation sold millions of books, from Arthur C. Clarke's *Childhood's End* to Marilyn Ferguson's *Aquarian Conspiracy*. People even started talking about The New Age. But not that many people. And some of those were snickering. *New Age* magazine carried too many ads making too many wild claims for the transformative powers of aging gurus, macrobiotic diets, magic crystals . . . The whole transformative thing became more than a little ridiculous.

As Lila discovered, the social goals of the sixties—an end to the war in Vietnam, an end to racism—gave way to more individual goals in the seventies and eighties. Get a job, make some money. Tom Wolfe wrote about "The Me Decade." Christopher Lasch weighed in with *The Culture of Narcissism*. Spike's time had arrived. Or was it that the times produced many Spikes? By the 1980s self-involvement became downright fashionable. In the great pinball game of life, more than a few of us ricocheted from the commitments of the sixties through the trials of the seventies to a selfishness of the eighties that seemed the very opposite of where we began. Let's review the bidding:

In the beginning, for the students of the sixties, was the Goal of graduation. But toward what further end? How to major, and why? Answer for ambitious engineers: beat the Russkies by mastering matter. Mathematics and physics offered an appropriate curriculum. But the mastery of matter did not solve all of the mysteries of the universe, so next came the Goal of wisdom. But my erstwhile idol, Heidegger, was very unwise about fascism. He fell hook, line and sinker for the final solution. And with my Hegelian quest for total understanding I might have done the same. Perhaps the high bar of a Ph.D. in philosophy was not, after all, equivalent to gaining the Goal of wisdom. The Goal of political justice seemed to me to set limits on the Prussian pursuit of the Goal of wisdom. Further, in the emergence of the New Left from the old left, justice was no longer viewed as a distant Goal distinct from the means of attaining it; instead the art of everyday life became part of a just livelihood that was an end in itself and not a means to some distant utopian Goal.

Through this series of goals—graduation, mastery over matter, wisdom, a just politics—the baby boom generation led the rest of American society on a kind of wild goose chase. First one Goal, then another, then yet another gave meaning to our lives and defined the relevant furniture of everyday life: first atoms and molecules, then philosophies, and then ideologies and the interests of the politically oppressed. But throughout the course of this wild Goal chase, one thing was never really in question: that the quest for some transcendent Goal was the best way to give meaning to one's life. Life had to have a purpose that was grounded in some form of absolute, whether political or spiritual. Otherwise life seemed meaningless. But as soon as we looked closely at those absolutes, they disappeared before our very eyes.

THE OBSOLESCENCE OF ABSOLUTES

During most of human history God was still in His heaven. There was a belief in some universal standard of right and wrong. Different cultures, different communities, different individuals, might have had differing beliefs about what that universal absolute standard was—and there lay the source of many a conflict. But the *idea* of such a standard was widely accepted. Groups and individuals may have differed over what they took to be the voice of the absolute, but the idea of a universal, hierarchical order with a single peak made sense to almost all.

When we come to history's postmodern act, the idea of an

absolute has already begun to fade. This erosion of the very idea of an absolute is different from the toppling of any particular candidate for the absolute. It is much more radical. This characteristically twentieth-century idea has arisen in several different contexts that bear no direct causal relationship to one another. A few will serve to illustrate what I mean by the erosion of absolutist thinking:

(1) Early in the century, Einstein's relativity theory demolished the concept of *absolute space*. Motion on a galactic scale cannot be plotted on some invisible but fixed grid that maps the universe. All motion must be measured relative to an observer, and that observer cannot claim to be absolutely motionless in absolute space. Space is no longer like some enormous room with a stable and knowable center.

(2) Einstein's theory also rendered obsolete *absolute simultaneity* in time. An idea as intuitively obvious as two people keeping rhythm by clapping together becomes relativized. Two events separated by light-years may appear simultaneous to one observer yet not to another.

(3) In international economics the gold standard served as a kind of *absolute wealth*. In 1972, Nixon took the United States off the gold standard. Since then we've been struggling with a system nicely named "the international float." Each currency is traded against all others. Though there have been various attempts to cobble together so-called "baskets" of several currencies to serve as a stable standard, there is nothing—not the dollar, not the Deutsche Mark,

not the yen—that functions as a financial absolute the way gold once did.

(4) In the political order a case could be made that the first half of the century was a struggle to see which nations would gain and hold *absolute sovereignty,* and the second half of the century has been about building a world order in which the very idea of absolute sovereignty has been eroded. Now there is an international "float" in political power that is increasingly grounded in economic rather than military might. Further, the very idea of national sovereignty is being challenged by the globalization of the economy and the establishment of trading blocs like the new Europe.

(5) Though some linguists still cling to the idea of a single "deep structure" lying beneath the surface differences among the world's many languages, the trend seems to be away from linguistic absolutes. Today's linguists live in a world where different natural languages—French, German, Italian, etc.— offer different approaches to translating *each other* in a kind of "linguistic float." There is no universal Esperanto worthy of the name, no single standard for all translation, least of all "reality." Rather than imagining that unambiguous *reference* can use reality as a gold standard, linguists and literary critics now speak of interpretations of interpretations of interpretations . . . with no certainty of ever finding semantic grounding in some absolute referent.

These five examples of the replacement of absolutist thinking—the demise of absolute space, absolute simultaneity, abso-

lute currency, absolute sovereignty, and absolute linguistic reference—have *not* hurled their respective disciplines into tailspins
of hopeless relativism. It is still possible to navigate in space
and time. The international economy still works. Some measure
of political power still exists, and people can still communicate
with one another without falling into hopeless confusion.

I cite these examples for two reasons: first, to give specific
and concrete content to the meaning of the decline of the
absolute; second, to quell the usual panic that sets in when
people confront the most obvious fissures in the absolute: the
death of God and the loss of a single standard of absolute
values.

Does the demise of the absolute mean despair is inevitable?
I don't think so. But to listen to the lamentations of some who
are sensitive to the closing of the modern era, you would think
we were witnessing a group funeral for the death of God, the
death of the self, the end of history, the death of national
sovereignty and the end of nature. Oh, woe! Oh, wringing of
hands! Where is the lyricism in *this* nihilism?

One of the principal features of postmodernism is the lack
of transcendent purpose or meaning. Goallessness and the postmodern deconstruction of authority go hand in hand: *not only*
has postmodernism come about because a lot of people have
lost faith in progress and are therefore running around without
Goals; *but also*, people who run around in postmodern times are
deprived of access to advice from reliable authorities when it
comes to making choices among their goals. Goals are not *given*
because in neither the historical dimension of purposeful action
nor the vertical dimension of some ladder to heaven can one
find an absolutely fixed target for taking aim at a Goal.

One's own individual actions cannot be justified by reference to some larger, collective Goal that can be read off the face of history. History no longer has a single face. History has been deconstructed into a tangled skein of alternative stories, various revisionisms, conflicting memories of our sometimes shared and sometimes disparate pasts. One, two, three, let a hundred histories bloom. Consequently, in postmodern times, the individual is deprived of a meaningful sense of history.

This multiplication of histories is the real meaning of Fukuyama's "end of history." The real point is not about the cessation of time and change but about the crowd of narratives that are oversimplified if woven too tightly into the single strand called History. The rope that was white, male, European history has become unraveled into a vast and tangled web that includes, but only with difficulty, the heritages of the Near and Far East, feminist history, as well as what little we know of the histories of Africa and South America, to say nothing of the timeless wisdom of Native Americans. The attempt to accommodate these different narratives in a single tale that includes European history as well is not easy. Today we no longer aspire to a totalizing view.

Without the old imperial confidence that we can speak to and for the totality of human history, the confrontation with other cultures becomes part of postmodernism—the realization that there are more than just a few ways to play the human game, and that American culture is not necessarily the most advanced, the highest, or the best. On the contrary, the triumphs of modernism might be a blight upon the face of the earth, a virus in the biosphere, an aberration in the long chain of evolutionary development that is now responsible for the disappearance of dozens of other species per wink of a cosmological eye. This recasting of the human species from the role of hero to the role of villain in the great historical drama leaves us without a hero for our own story, and hence with no convincing story.

The point about the end of history is to digest, fully and completely, the message of postmodernism, namely (in the words of one of the French pundits of postmodernism, Jean François Lyotard) that there is "no convincing metanarrative," no all-embracing story line, no single plot with a happy outcome to satisfy our need for a Goal or our sense of an ending. And that is disturbing. It is not disturbing because the end is not happy. It is disturbing because there is no end at all, no tidy conclusion, no final Goal, no closure. Things just keep happening.

THE LACK OF a cosmic metanarrative resonates in our daily lives as the reawakening of a sense of mystery. To know that you cannot possibly imagine where you will be in ten years' time, that no sense of place can provide a stable background for your dreams of movement, no fixed ladder, no map of the familiar, no chart of known waters exists that would allow you to navigate with certainty from the present to that future—this is to be truly and deeply adrift in time and without a clue to what the distant future will look like.

What does it feel like, not only to have no stable home but to suspect that you will never have a stable home? What does it feel like to surrender all attachment to domesticity? To give up hopes of a hearth where the same Christmas stockings hang for years running? What is it like to surrender all fantasies of long dinner tables crowded with close friends who talk with one another day in and day out? Can one completely neglect the web they used to call community? What is it like to know that all of your dinner partners are acquaintances, not friends, and that your loyalties are limited, despite whatever confidences are exchanged over coffee? To be so adrift is to be at risk. To lack any goal at all is to be aimless.

Of course we can each set our own individual goals: to climb Mount Everest, to write a novel, to raise a family. But these individual goals, whatever they may be, no longer find their justification in some larger pattern provided by a coherent picture of historical progress. So we find ourselves making it up as we go along, more or less the way an artist creates. We can have our local goals, but they are not easy to locate on some larger map. *This* is the significance of the loss of absolutes.

For Love of Narcissus

Narcissism accompanies all the strata of our experience, independently of them. In other words, it is not only an immature stage of life needing to be superseded, but also the ever renewing companion of all of life.

—Lou Andreas Salome

4

THE SEVENTIES WERE SOBERING. The scientific goals of the fifties and the social goals of the sixties both shared the nobility of self-sacrifice. Not so the goals of the seventies and eighties. Self-realization is the very opposite of self-sacrifice. And greed . . . well, hold the nobility while we count the cash.

A strong identity is the tacit goal of those who turn away from society in order to "find themselves." But the model of artistic self-creation suggests that the self is no more *found*, like some preexisting *thing*, than a picture is found on a blank canvas. The "identity crisis" is no longer a stage through which adolescents pass just once, but a perpetual condition. Self-creation is never done.

BECAUSE THERE ARE costs to the spreading of individualism, a strong back eddy now curls upstream against the centuries-old current toward self-awareness. Especially in the land of rampant individualism, the United States of America, one hears voices rising in alarm against the dangers of too much individualism. One hears complaints about creeping narcissism.

I try to put these notes of alarm in perspective by recalling the details of the ancient myth in its own innocent purity. After taking up the charges that have been leveled against the heirs of Narcissus, I acknowledge the nonsense of narcissism and *the fruitlessness of taking self-actualization as one's Goal*. But the *non-sense* will be evident only after the *sense* is apparent. It is worth acknowledging that the turn toward the Goal of self-realization is not an accident but an understandable reaction to historical circumstances—an inward Goal that is meant to substitute for the loss of outer Goals.

The times are changing. The old political and religious absolutes have been eroded by the history of the twentieth century and we individuals have been thrown back on our own devices. We can no longer organize our lives by hanging them on the Goals that were justified by religious or political ideals. But we can do better than Spike's retreat into body building.

Rather than learning to swim in the rapids of the twentieth century, many have chosen to grasp what they take to be the rocks of their own private lives. Like Spike, they learn to look out for number one. They become selfish. I find this reaction as abhorrent as the resignation that wants to settle for the goals of a functionary. But it is an understandable reaction given the turbulence of the times.

Subjectivity—the experience of selfhood—is not immune to history, however much recent history may be driving individuals into the cocoons of their own privacy where they might think they can isolate themselves from history. Like subjectivity, madness, too, has a history. Each culture, each era, has its own way of driving people crazy.

In Victorian society, hysteria was the mental illness of choice. This is why so much of Freud's work is oriented toward hysterical neuroses. Around the middle of the twentieth century, schizophrenia picked up in popularity. By the 1970s and '80s, however, "borderline narcissistic personality disorders" became the preferred presenting symptoms in many psychiatrists' offices.

The momentum of recent history leads toward the solitude of Narcissus, who abandons all goals outside his grotto, even love. This is unfortunate, and unnecessary. But until one appreciates the sources of narcissism in these changing postmodern times, the regrettable aspects of this tendency toward narcissism will remain cloaked under the secrecy imposed by guilt. So let us follow the trajectory from the public to the private, from the old Goals of religion and politics to the new Goal of self-actualization. Let us follow Narcissus into his grotto and see whether it is possible to come out the other side singing.

WHAT IS THE connection between the history of madness and the history of subjectivity? And how has the flowering of narcissism been conditioned by our entry into the information era? What can the culture of postmodernism tell us about the influences on subjectivity in the late twentieth century? A quick review of some of the main points in the movement from modernism to postmodernism in art, architecture and literary criticism will reveal some themes sufficient to make the narcissistic personality feel right at home.

Modernism in architecture includes works from Mies van der Rohe and the Bauhaus school to the glass boxes produced by Skidmore, Owings and Merrill. Modernist architecture looks mechanical in its regularity, functionality and impersonality. Postmodern architecture, by contrast, is playful, ironic and eclectic—a Doric column here, a Victorian embellishment there, an unpredictable assemblage of elements from the entire grab bag of past, present and future. It is as if buildings themselves had learned to mix and match their wardrobes like a woman who shops at Armani one day and CostCo the next. Postmodern architecture differs from modern architecture much as the more playful New Left differed from the more earnest old.

Literary modernism, as exemplified in the work of T. S. Eliot and works like *The Wasteland,* is a reaction to impersonality and meaninglessness. Postmodernism in literature is the province more of critics than of authors. The earmarks of postmodern literary criticism include attempts to challenge the authority of the author. The reader and the critic determine the reception of the literary work of art. The author is a barely self-conscious site where social, economic, historical and psychological influences meet and intersect.

Like the authority of the author, the autonomy of the self becomes suspect in the postmodern era. The single captain of the ship, the solitary ego at the helm of the self, has been deconstructed into a complex play of social, psychological, economic and historical forces. Rather than take the author as an autonomous *origin* of a text that is supposed to express the author's intentions, Edward Said substitutes the word "beginnings" for "origins" in order to undercut the image of author as a godlike creator for whom everything turns out as intended or foreordained.

Just as an author is not the origin or god of a text, so the self is not an all-powerful god over its life. Just as a beginning is not necessarily a godlike origin, so an end is not necessarily a goal. Nietzsche's "goallessness as such" amounts to a deconstruction of the idea of Fate or Destiny in a way that mirrors Said's substitution of beginnings for origins.

The forces at play in the serial construction of a self are not mechanical, not mere pushes and pulls or attractions and repulsions. Instead postmodernity is *a symbolic arena* that functions not according to the laws of physics but according to the rules of grammar, syntax and semantics. What's more, many postmodernists doubt whether signs can be unambiguously tied down to a physical reality.

Both in art and architecture, postmodernism exhibits an ironic detachment from stolid functionality or steadfast representation. Narrow interpretations of *utility* give way to whimsical display. Abhorrence of photographic representation in art gives way to ironic repetitions of repetitions. What is Reality? Who knows? More important, who cares? The scientific quest for Truth has given way to a sometimes desperate, sometimes ironic search for *Meaning.* Truth, in a narrow literal sense, is not at issue. Both the story and the joke are narrative forms that rely on strings of symbols to create meaning—without necessarily relying on truth. Quite to the contrary, novels are fictions, and jokes turn on ambiguities or double meanings.

The information and service sectors of the postmodern economy are as different from the mass-manufacturing modern economy as postmodern art and criticism are from their modernist predecessors—and in some of the same ways. Instead of relying on the tool and die shop of mechanical reproduction, the postmodern arts rely on the rag and bone shop of the imagination. Instead of relying on literal repetition and slavish representation of the *same,* the information and service sectors of the postmodern economy call for innovation and customization of the *different.*

A primary function of technology in industrial mass manufacturing was *repetition*—the repeated production of more and more of *the same thing* by way of *standardization.* The function of technology in an information economy is just the opposite: *innovation*—differentiations that make a difference. This key difference between the basic functions of technology in industrial and information economies is fundamental, as stark as the difference between sameness and difference. And this difference *changes everything, undercutting one of the central goals of industrial capitalism:* the accumulation of more of the same.

Most important for our understanding of Goallessness, in a world where the creation of the different prevails over accumulation of the same, the scales used for measuring self-worth have to shift. A cattleman can afford to be modest. The biggest ranchers in Texas will admit to having "a few cows," because they know their physical wealth can be counted, and will not disappear overnight. Not so with admen in New York or agents in Hollywood, where hype is everything. The levels of politics and interpersonal skills are notoriously low in the academic world because the people there have so little that is physical and tangible to show for their achievements. Consequently they become just a little desperate about their self-esteem. You meet more narcissists among scholars and writers than among carpenters and bricklayers. Why? It is not just a matter of economics. Rather, it is a question of *the solidity of the medium in which one works.*

One has to be impressed by the sheer volatility of wealth that is based on information rather than on land, labor or physical capital. Once upon a time you knew the size of an estate, you could count the size of a herd, you could weigh the quantity of gold and walk off the acres of land. And none of these quantities was likely to jump discontinuously from one day to the next. Physical quantities vary continuously by increments of gradual addition and subtraction. Not so with quantities that are determined by intangibles like popularity, credit, exchange rates, interest rates, reputations or sudden changes in financial or show-biz market values. Over the past decade we have witnessed remarkable reversals of fortune among men like Donald Trump, Michael Jackson, and Michael Milken. Mighty empires have been brought down "overnight": Chrysler, E. F. Hutton. Paper is more volatile than gold, and electronic blips on data tapes yet more volatile still. And fame or reputation more ephemeral than fixed capital. This makes the business landscape in the information era an intrinsically dangerous and risky place to play. You can't count on solid foundations. The transfiguration of black ink into red is a perpetual possibility when one gets into the leveraging game. Risk is real.

This new skittishness at the core of what Freud so glibly called the "Reality Principle" is enough to induce the wildest of oscillations in a person's sense of self-worth. And it is precisely this oscillation that is characteristic of narcissism. It is wrong, as we shall see, to think of narcissists as *only* in love with themselves.

The current epidemic of narcissism is an altogether natural reaction to the lack of security people experience in the contemporary cultural and economic environment. Once the old navigational aids have been abandoned there is a danger of dizziness, the vertigo of freedom. As they say in Hollywood, you're only as good as your last movie. An inventory of innovation, like a wagonload of ripe fruit, rots in real time. Consequently there is a tendency toward self-inflation and grandiosity among the purveyors of such perishables.

If success in a symbolic universe is, as they say, mostly smoke and mirrors, then Spike and the rest of us have to learn how to look in the mirror. And if we *must* be narcissists, we might as well get good at it. So that is why the rest of this chapter is about getting *good* at narcissism. Some Goals are easily abandoned by a simple act of letting go. But the Goal of self-actualization is so alluring, the temptations of the precious self so enticing as an alternative to the causes that defined the Goals of the sixties and seventies, that we are swimming in narcissistic waters. It won't do to say, "Give up the Goal of self-actualization." A subtler, more counterintuitive therapy is called for: one that swims toward the Goal of self-actualization, only to discover its evanescence.

Rather than condemning narcissism as bad or elevating it as good, we need to understand the general phenomenon of narcissism as historically and culturally conditioned by our entry into the postmodern information era. Then we can get on with the task of separating out the socially and personally debilitating aspects of narcissism from other aspects that might offer some hope for learning to live without the Grand Goals provided by politics or religion.

THE FLOWERING OF
NARCISSUS

According to ancient myth, Narcissus spurned the company of others. He preferred gazing at his own reflection in a pool of water. He fell in love with his reflection, so totally that he neglected everyone and everything else, from Echo, his spurned lover, to the nourishment of food. He starved to death upon the bank by the water, and there, where his rotting body mulched the soil, grew the flower with a golden heart we now know as Narcissus.

The details of the myth are worth recalling, for many Americans in the nineties are knee-deep in narcissism, a word much on the lips of social critics Daniel Bell, Christopher Lasch, Richard Sennett and Robert Bellah. The flowering of narcissism is a sign that some postmoderns have finally found their way in the solitary wilderness that modernists used to call alienation. Narcissism is a reaction to the condition we used to call alienation before we learned how to live with it. Narcissists are just those who have been alienated long enough to learn to love it, or at least like it (love with irony).

To suggest this slant on narcissism is to take a more upbeat tempo on what others play as a dirge. According to their accounts, our public life and our community spirit have fallen prey to a passion for privacy and the seductions of the precious self. Political devotions have given way to personal concerns. The burgeoning human potentials movement has stolen the fire from the social conscience of the sixties. "The Me Decade" is the title of an essay by Tom Wolfe, whose lighter step still accelerates other critics toward a gathering crescendo in a solemn mass for modern society: narcissism is a Bad Thing.

Perhaps. But universally agreed-upon Bad Things in social history have a funny way of promoting cures worse than the disease, viz., the Victorian and Puritan repressions of sexuality. Venus/Aphrodite, the goddess of beauty and sexuality, was exiled from the Victorian pantheon. But the exiled have an uncanny way of returning as martyrs.

Narcissism can be pathological, to be sure. But instead of calling for quarantine or cure we might do well to look more closely at the relationships between symptom and cause, and, second, at the implications of the diagnosis. For the first step we are much indebted to the critics. They have seen that narcissism is not just an epidemic among individuals who have been careless about their mental hygiene. Narcissism, though individualized in its solitary symptoms, is a *social* problem with social causes and social effects. But I reject the critics' invitation to stamp out creeping narcissism right down to its insidious social roots. We ought to be wary of attempts to exterminate weeds of whatever kind. Let's bring a little ecological consciousness to our culture as well as to nature. Let's find the niche where Narcissus belongs and appreciate the meaning of his overstepping that niche. These imbalances do not just happen by accident. Perhaps there is something to be learned in a respect for this latest cultural pathology. Narcissism is not *all* bad.

What defense can I offer without romanticizing and thereby spreading this "social disease"? This is the rub: the attempt to appreciate a residue of health in the narcissistic personality will be confused with an excuse for more dreaded self-indulgence and egotistical self-aggrandizement. We don't want to encourage petty selfishness. If we're all looking out for *numero uno,* none of us will enjoy the shared benefits that social endeavors offer. That point is elementary. The subtler question is how to nourish social bonds in a neighborhood of narcissists without exiling or exterminating its residents. We need more understanding than antipathy. Hatred will hardly handle a syndrome whose origin is the lack of love.

Narcissism Degree Zero

Psychoanalysts distinguish between primary and secondary narcissism. *Primary* narcissism exhibits the relative innocence of a childlike self-love that is almost oblivious of otherness. *Secondary* narcissism is a less innocent, more egotistical self-love that follows a choice between love of *self* and love of a clearly distinguished *other.*

I want to describe a state I will call *tertiary narcissism.* It is even less innocent than secondary narcissism. It's what you get when you take a secondary narcissist like Spike, scold him for his narcissism and make him guilty about loving himself. Tertiary narcissism is *so* guilty that it refuses to accept itself as narcissism. It is a preoccupation with self without an appreciation of self. It takes the form of a torpor untouchable by others, a withdrawal into a flat, colorless indisposition. Tertiary narcissism is self-love locked in coitus with self-hatred. It represents all of the dilemmas of narcissism and none of the delights. It is a box canyon from which there is no escape, a vacant interiority entered from fear of the outside, a barren place where the self can find no joy, for, as we are all supposed to know, self-love is a Bad Thing.

My major difference with the current critics of narcissism is that, failing to distinguish between potentially constructive and obviously destructive elements of narcissism, they would herd all narcissists, primary and secondary alike, straight into the box canyon of tertiary narcissism from which, as I have said, there is no escape. But if it is impossible to go beyond tertiary narcissism, what about backing up? What about reversing direction, back through the egotism of the secondary stage, back through the childlike innocence of the primary stage, to an even "earlier" stage I'll call *narcissism degree zero?* Examples? Muhammad Ali, who proclaims to the world, "I am the greatest"; the audacity of a Norman Mailer, who writes a book called *Advertisements for Myself.*

Narcissism degree zero achieves a benign annihilation of self through a self-involvement so thorough that the nothingness, the *nihil* at the heart of self, cannot fail to be discovered. Narcissism degree zero swallows its own navel. By setting itself high on a pedestal of exhibitionistic display, narcissism degree zero renders itself purposely vulnerable to incendiary laughter and ridicule. It is a dangerous game that deconstructs the Goal of self-realization even as it appears to construct a monumental ego.

Several examples demonstrate the syndrome of a T. Nietzsche titles chapters of his autobiography "Why I Am So Wise" and "Why I Write Such Good Books." Roland Barthes includes pictures of himself and samples of his inconsequential doodles in his *Roland Barthes by Roland Barthes*. In these examples we can see a kind of *goofing on the precious self.*

This patently self-conscious wallowing in self-adulation turns out to be a *reductio ad absurdum* of preoccupations with self. By their fancy footwork, their shifts of field, their revelations of self-contradiction, these zeroed-out narcissists demonstrate to one and all—themselves included—the *insubstantiality of self.* To see how they escape from the abject aimlessness that Spike fell into, let's take a closer look at a few of the pros and how they have done it.

In *Genius and Lust, A Journey Through the Major Writings of Henry Miller,* Norman Mailer follows Henry Miller through the metamorphoses of his psychosexual development as an author. The central pathology is, of course, narcissism, but not the kind you read about in Freudian texts. Mailer notes the route to self-annihilation by observing, "one can detest oneself intimately and still be a narcissist. What characterizes narcissism is the fundamental relation. It is with oneself. The same dialectic of love and hate that mates feel for one another is experienced within the self."

The self is internally pluralized into two, or possibly into several selves. "The inner dialogue hardly ever ceases," writes Mailer, and we might justly ask him whether this active inner dialogue of the narcissist is not the stuff of which his novels are made. Mailer knows Miller's narcissism so well because Mailer's relationship with himself allows him insight. In short, much of Mailer on Miller is actually Mailer on Mailer. He even gives us a lesson in displaced reading of displaced writing: he tells us to read Anaïs Nin's writing on their shared lover, June, as Nin on Miller.

"Curious!" writes Mailer. "If we fix on Miller's mind rather than June's beauty, Nin could be giving a description of his talent: *startling, burning, phosphorescent, bizarre, fantastic, nervous, in high fever . . .*" each of these terms lifted from a long quotation from Nin on June. Mailer carries on: ". . . full of *color, brilliance* and finally *lacking the courage of its personality,* leaving behind *chaos* and *whirlpools of feeling.* Yet it may be all a *pose.* One *cannot grasp the core"* . . . of June, of Henry Miller, of Norman Mailer. A bit confusing, but if we pick up the rhythm of ironic resonance, Mailer's essay on Miller turns out to be Mailer on Nin on Mailer on . . .

THE PERFORMING SELF (the title of a highly relevant book by Richard Poirer) is aware of his own performance *as* a performance. The appearance of this performance need not represent some singular true self *behind* the performance. Again, ostensibly describing Miller, Mailer writes: "He comes to discover all those modern themes which revolve around the discovery of oneself. Soon he will dive into the pit of recognizing that there may not be a geological fundament in the psyche one can call identity." Through discovering the lack of a singular substantial self, Mailer discovers the vanity of the Goal of self-realization.

In Mailer's discourse on Miller we see that the sober assumption of singular selfhood simply cannot approximate the experience of narcissism degree zero. It is not a question of ego; not even of *monumental* ego, for the truly self-conscious narcissist *knows* the extent of his act, and in that knowledge the monument burns into nothingness . . . or crumbles into a multiplicity of fragmentary personalities. There is no possibility of recollecting those shards of identity into a new unity. Miller and Mailer have abandoned forever that "geological fundament"; they have broached into a sea where the usual assumptions about selfhood hold no water.

"What Miller has bogged into . . . is the uncharted negotiations of the psyche when two narcissists take the vow of love." Here we find not a self in search of its singular identity but whole casts of characters in search of an audience rather than an author. "The narcissist is not self-absorbed so much as one self is absorbed in studying the other. The narcissist is the scientist and the experiment in one. Other people exist for their ability to excite one presence or another in oneself." Further, on the inflammatory conjunction of exhibitionistic narcissists in love, "Promiscuity is the happy opportunity to try a new role."

By dint of the sheer excess that is inevitable on the route to narcissism degree zero, the wild reversal from solitude to promiscuity makes a certain crazy sense. We are, after all, swimming in the waters of what psychiatrists call "primary process," the dreamland of the unconscious where white becomes black, the way up becomes the way down, and 180-degree reversals of sign are far more common than lesser modifications of direction. *Of course* promiscuity will be the way narcissists enter the field of love if they ever leave their private grottoes.

There is a link between promiscuity and the fragmentary dissolution of the ego on its descent into narcissism degree zero. Promiscuity is a way of acting out a profligacy of eros, a squandering of one's capacity for attachment which is at once risky (for who knows where it will lead?) and safe (since a devotion to *one* other love demands far more vulnerability than promiscuity).

This same link between fragmentation and the profligacy of narcissism degree zero is evident in the aphoristic style of some of the world's great philosophical narcissists: Pascal, Kierkegaard, Nietzsche, Wittgenstein. Another aphorist, Randall Reid, once wrote, "An aphorism on aphorisms: they are the mark of a promiscuous mind. An aphorist avoids philosophy as a roué avoids marriage; he is afraid to commit himself." Further: "I write by fits and starts, flirting with subjects as promiscuously as if they were women. *Scriptus interruptus.*"

The author of *Writing Degree Zero* and *The Pleasure of the Text,* Roland Barthes, shows all the same signs: exhibitionism (just look at his autobiography), an aphoristic style and an explicit awareness of the fragmentary diffusion of his selfhood. "To write by fragments: the fragments are then so many stones on the perimeter of a circle: I spread myself around: my whole little universe in crumbs; at the center, what?"

So uncertain is the point of origin, lacking a "geological fundament" called *I,* Barthes's voice continually shifts back and forth from first person to third: "Liking to find, to write *beginnings,* he [writing about himself] tends to multiply this pleasure: that is why he writes fragments: so many fragments, so many beginnings, so many pleasures; but he doesn't like the ends: the risk of rhetorical clausule is too great: the fear of not being able to resist the *last word.*" Barthes is not the least interested in attaining some literary Goal. It is enough to keep beginning.

Barthes describes his process of beginning: "I begin producing by reproducing the person I want to be." This production, or reproduction, is not guided by some singular, authoritative captain of the ship. Writing under the title, "The person divided?"—"You are a patchwork of reactions: is there anything *primary* in you?" Finally—but not for Roland Barthes, who abhors final closure—he compares himself to "a disintegrating statue or an eroding relief, its shape blurs and fades, or better still, like Harpo Marx losing his artificial beard in the glass of water he is drinking out of."

Thus does the grandiose narcissist of degree zero agree to play the fool and carry out before his own and everyone else's eyes this goof on ego. Thus does the egotism of aiming at the

Goal of self-actualization in secondary and primary narcissism allow itself to disintegrate in the Goallessness of narcissism degree zero.

WHEN NARCISSISM TAKES to the stage or silver screen, it shows its truest colors, and then fades in an evanescence that is the best portrayal of the insubstantiality of the self. In the Narcissus story's symbol of the mirrored image lies an important truth about the self, a truth that is part of the saving remnant of ineradicable narcissism. *Subjectivity is not a substance.* It is not a material thing with fixed dimensions and qualities. *The self is a process of reflection,* one that lacks a substantial, originary core. Instead it is a kind of elevation by the bootstraps, a reflection of reflections of reflections whose origins are equally evanescent.

Subjectivity is not some self-identical *thing,* but a process that must always be reflecting itself at a distance from itself. *Fame* is the mirror in which zero degree narcissists aspire to see their image reflected. But setting fame as a Goal demands that one leave the confines of literal privacy. The pursuit of narcissism degree zero then becomes its own therapy. When privacy goes public it is, inevitably, less private. Granted, the achievement of the Goal of fame is no substitute for intimacy. One does not enjoy the kind of give and take with a TV audience that one has with a close companion. But public recognition is recognition by *some* other, and that's at least a beginning for self-consciousness.

Hegel put it this way: "Self-consciousness exists in itself and for itself, in that, and by the fact that, it exists for another self-consciousness; that is to say, it *is* only by being acknowledged or 'recognized.'" More simply, there is a certain Tinkerbell effect for self-consciousness. You remember Peter Pan's little sidekick whose life and light threatened to flicker out unless the audience clapped. We're all a little like that. No wonder we try to drum up a little of our own applause from time to time. But . . . modesty forbids it.

And so do the social critics. Our cultural heritage bears ambivalences toward what the Buddhists call "self-existent delight." On the one hand, American culture builds on an individualist tradition in which salvation is personal rather than tribal; on the other hand, egalitarians take offense when any particular person places himself above others. The rights and liberties of the individual are sacred, yet the individual who promotes her own rights is somehow pushy. To some extent the social critics are right, but one is left in the end with an uneasy sense of being counterproductively scolded.

American culture can't lead people to narcissistic waters and expect them not to drink in their reflections on its surface. American culture can't spend billions on advertising that tries to cultivate glittering self-images, and then snatch away the mirror when political party enrollments drop. Rather than admonishing people, as does Harvard sociologist Daniel Bell, with puritanical attacks against "self-aggrandizement," the social critics might accomplish much more by becoming *social enthusiasts*—pied pipers who would lure narcissists out of their privacy rather than lash them back into the box canyon of tertiary narcissism. The antinarcissist dirge does not inspire us to dance along. It is a funeral procession for eighteenth- and nineteenth-century utopian values.

NARCISSISTS, UNITE!

A positive alternative to narcissism today must draw its power and appeal from some of the same social forces that make narcissism itself so popular. The outworn ethic of the eighteenth-century Enlightenment, the idealizations of *community*, will not do. *Differentiation* is the name of the game this century, in the era of information: *differences that make a difference.* The quest for identity proceeds not by identification with all mankind but by shared differentiations: *we* wear pin-stripe suits, *we* shave our heads, *we* ride motor scooters, *we* love Garfield the Cat.

Taken to its extreme, which is the way social movements usually announce themselves most clearly, this process of differentiation devolves from *we* to *me.* Lord Byron and other nineteenth-century dandies were high culture's anticipations of a trend that has by now lowered its heavy brow. Now almost everyone can afford an identity crisis, not just the elite who could read Goethe's *Sorrows of Young Werther.* But to see the cultural spread of this process only in its most salient form—that is, in terms of isolated, increasingly narcissistic *individuals* like Howard Hughes—is to miss the significance of a closely related phenomenon: social bonding based on a shared pride in *differentness.*

There are many communities of shared interests. Their multiplicity is not a sign that we have fallen from some condition of uniform grace; instead it is a sign that we have evolved beyond total dependence upon the uniformities of nature. We have exercised reason and imagination whose products are not, nor should they be, everywhere the same. Human beings, singly and in groups, are figuring out different ways to make up the human game as they go along. That's all right. It's called freedom. It is artful. It is the practice of living without a Goal.

Narcissism is an extreme and ultimately self-defeating form of the broad historical trend toward increasing differentiation and articulation of the human spirit. Once understood as *too much of a good thing* rather than as an unmitigated Bad Thing, then the flowering of narcissism offers some hope for learning to live without a predestined Goal.

The historical trends that gave us narcissism can support islands of solidarity as well. When you follow narcissism degree zero toward the insubstantiality of self, you see that self-love must finally spread itself across the social pattern of reflections that constitute the self. When privacy goes public you see the self as a pattern of relations of mutual recognition. The celebration of self becomes a song for the ears of the other, not for the sake of self-aggrandizement but for the benefit of shared acts of artful self-creation.

The myth of Narcissus now yields a new significance. Rather than marking a dead end, narcissism reveals itself as a transition. The myth, after all, is a story of death and transfiguration. Even primary and secondary narcissism, if pursued through their course, have a necessary half-life. Like Spike, the mythical Narcissus, or the real Howard Hughes, whatever part of us wills total solitude must literally or metaphorically starve and die. Because the postmodern self is like a polytheistic pantheon with several personages, several stories, the culmination of one's Narcissus need not require the literal death of one's entire internal pantheon of personalities.

Though the real threats of narcissism are not to be minimized or excused, the way out might lie with replaying the drama back to its innocent origins at degree zero: with an

acceptance, affirmation and enactment of self-love. We can survive the inevitable death of that part of ourselves that would
seek solitary gratification, for there is more to each of us than
one story line, one plot.

The worst that can happen to the narcissistic personality is
paralysis. There is no point in keeping Narcissus from his pool.
Where else will the limitations of his character be revealed to
him? If the chorus of criticism against narcissism pretends to be
a therapy, it sounds rather like punishing parents complaining
to daughter over the dinner table: "Don't play anorexic with
me! Eat up!" This is not good therapy.

Rather than lamenting narcissism with the dirge, let's kick
out the jams with a New Orleans wake for the *useful self* with its
slave mentality and rock-solid ego. I want to see T-shirts pro-
claiming, *"I'm a narcissist, and proud of it!"* Narcissists of the world,
unite! You have nothing to lose but your narcissism. And to
gain?

Groves of golden hearts.

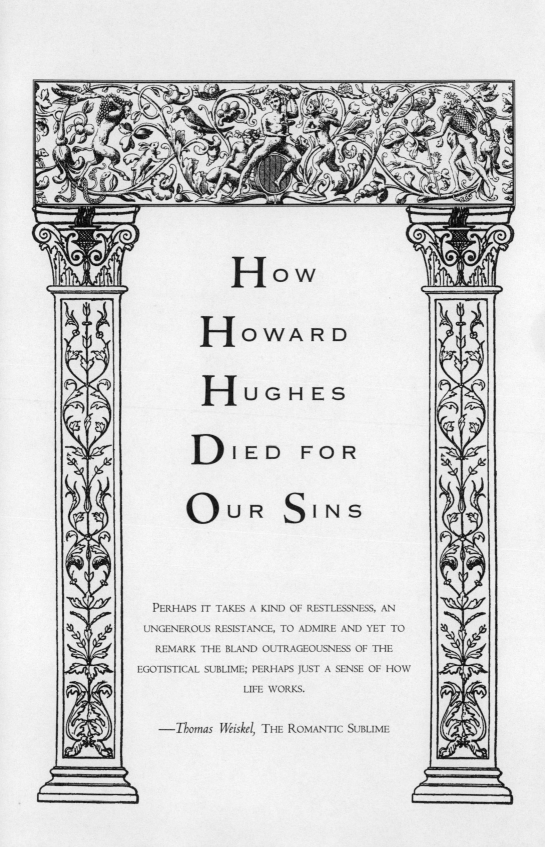

How Howard Hughes Died for Our Sins

Perhaps it takes a kind of restlessness, an ungenerous resistance, to admire and yet to remark the bland outrageousness of the egotistical sublime; perhaps just a sense of how life works.

—*Thomas Weiskel*, The Romantic Sublime

5

FTER HUGHES'S DEAD BODY was removed from his last hotel suite in Acapulco, aides dismantled the movie screen, projector and sound system. "There were no other personal belongings of Hughes to be taken care of," writes James Phelan, in *Howard Hughes: The Hidden Years*. "He had no photographs, no mementos, no favorite paintings, no cherished books, none of the sentimental impediments that people normally carry with them from place to place. The man whose holdings defied comprehension did not own any clothes—just a bathrobe, an old fashioned Stetson snap-brim hat, a couple of pairs of pajamas, and a small supply of specially made shorts equipped with drawstrings. His long litany of taboos included shorts fitted with buttons or metal snaps. He did not own any clothes because he did not wear clothes. For more than ten years he had shuffled about his blacked-out bedrooms naked or clothed only in his drawstring shorts."

None of the sentimental impediments . . . ! How could Howard Hughes, who "had everything," end up with nothing? Or, to turn this tragedy on its head and find a lesson for the rest of us in this epic life and death, how does the tale of Howard Hughes help us to follow the logic of the death and transfiguration of Narcissus, not just as a mythological abstraction but as a concrete narrative of the twentieth-century attempt to gain control over one's life?

In this chapter I want to focus on the "outrageousness of the egotistical sublime" as it is demonstrated in the life of Howard Hughes. The following chapters say more about "how life works." The point is to appreciate the forces that drive a guy toward narcissism when the furniture of everyday life gets remodeled from *things* with their relatively sharp boundaries to *symbols* that are both sublime and intrinsically ambiguous. Hughes's story demonstrates in high relief the contradictions of his age: materialism and narcissism in the twilight of the industrial era. Speed, privacy, flight, beauty, Hollywood, wealth . . . he not only played the major tunes of America's twentieth century, *he helped score them.*

His life was exemplary in ways that make him worth monitoring as an early warning system for the rest of us in our pursuit of Goals which, if we could see them more clearly realized, we might not want. He achieved the Goals of wealth and fame and power but died a hermit's death. Locked for his last years behind the high walls of a self-imposed exile from other people, he literally withered away for fear of being contaminated by some alien thing.

Like Howard Hughes—and here lies his value as an early warning system—the zero degree narcissist lives in danger, because narcissism is potentially fatal. Though usually found in the form of a chronic, low-level solitude that is expert at hiding from public scrutiny, narcissism can nonetheless flare up at any time and suck all the world into the flame of the individual ego. Nice people, pillars of the community, can suddenly disappear from the usual meetings only to be found weeks later, surrounded by mounds of videocassettes, rumpled sheets, and the crumbs of countless kinds of junk food. They have succumbed to the combined lures of Hollywood and their own company, an almost unbeatable combination in parts of today's world like Los Angeles or Manhattan or Lost Fork, Montana.

Hughes's story is instructive just to the extent that he demonstrates the dangers of arrested development in traversing the narrow pass through narcissism degree zero. He was a master at the economics of the sublime: he built his fortune on speed (the airline industry) and entertainment (the movie industry)—both of which are more sublime than material. But in the end he was defeated by his passion for *control.*

How did his pursuit of speed and beauty and wealth and fame lead to slow decline into existential poverty and reclusiveness? *Goal-directed behavior and instrumental rationality,* that's how. On an almost mythic scale Hughes demonstrates the dangers of a kind of goal-directed mentality that tries to exercise in the realm of the sublime the instrumental manipulation and control that were once appropriate in the realm of material things. Howard Hughes got caught, before the rest of us, with one leg in the industrial era and one leg in the information era, and the confusion consumed him.

HUGHES INHERITED A modest fortune from his father, who had founded Hughes Tool Company. Hughes used the resources of the tool company to build airplanes. He flew as his own test pilot, broke speed records and survived several near fatal crashes. He became one of the architects of the airline industry by founding and building TWA. As if one major career were not enough, he also built a reputation as a Hollywood tycoon, movie producer and star maker.

But these are just the facts. Far more interesting are the quirks: his passion for privacy; his crazy hours that would keep him awake for long stretches of manic activity; the way he would call colleagues at all hours of the night; his mysterious disappearances, like the time he took a job as a lowly baggage handler for the airline he owned.

Clues to his character can be found by looking at how and where he chose to spend his time during his "disappearances." For example, how to interpret the fact that he and a friend flew around the Southwest for weeks performing touch-and-go landings at isolated little airfields? A partial answer: there is a lure of impersonality that the Southwest exerts on the narcissistic personality. You can see it in the scenes around the oil rigs in the film *Five Easy Pieces*. You can see it in Jean Baudrillard's book, *America*, where the lure of the open road through the desert is as strong as in any text since Kerouac's *On the Road*. Another brother of the narcissistic fraternity, the Lone Ranger, doesn't take to his saddle in the Southwest for nothing. It is a place where one can easily avoid the pain of *others.*

HOWARD HUGHES WORSHIPED at the altars of speed and beauty . . . and money. What could be more twentieth-century American? He enjoyed many women and died alone. He became fabulously wealthy and, like King Midas, lost the ability to savor his wealth. He could have anything he wanted, and ended up hiring Mormons—because they were the only ones he would trust—to catch flies and remove them from his room with gloved hands and Kleenex.

He also needed staff to run the movie projector. Decades before the invention of the VCR, Hughes was a pioneer in the practice of watching movies as an audience of one. He withdrew into his prototype electronic grotto to sit alone and watch old movies long before the time of videotapes. What is now so easy for millions to do he accomplished by having his own projector. Stacks of bulky thirty-five-millimeter film cans cluttered his room. When people discovered at the time of his death that he had indulged himself in orgies of old movies, they regarded this unheard-of practice as a clear sign of madness. *What? Watch a movie alone? You watch movies in movie theaters. You watch television alone.* Today we cannot cast the stone of madness so quickly without risking our own glass houses now that most households have a videocassette recorder. Many now know the pleasures that Hughes indulged. His "madness" has been democratized by the advent of the VCR.

Long before people started using the word "cocooning"

Howard Hughes was hanging around the house all day in his pajamas. People are doing this today, not just the idle rich, but workers who come home to what the demographers call "single person households," which numbered almost 23 million in 1990, up 25% since 1980. For the first time in the history of humanity many people are living utterly alone, isolated from the tribe. What do they do with themselves, completely removed from the gaze of others? How do they spend their time? What clothes do they wear when no one else will see them? What indulgences do they allow themselves? What amusements do they engage in? What forms of self-gratification?

This is where the frontier of humanity is being decided: in millions of private lives where the art of carving the near edge of the future is being practiced by millions of amateur artists now liberated by isolation from the disapproving gaze of *others*. Not in public spaces, not in treaties and contracts, not in physical shapes built of bricks and mortar or steel and plastic, but in private places where people give free rein to their imaginations—there they fill their time with conversation on the telephone with friends, or with TV, or movies on the VCR, or gardening or exercise or any number of other things they like to do at home. What are those things? Here we will find answers to the questions we might have about the future of the human species. And here, in the private grotto of twentieth-century narcissism, Howard Hughes was a pioneer, a test pilot in the sublime skies of privacy.

But Hughes crashed.

Why?

THE PASSION FOR CONTROL

Hughes treated people—especially beautiful women—the same way he treated airplanes: with a passion for perfection and control that runs contrary to the way life works. One of the lessons to be learned from Howard Hughes is this: the instrumental rationality that pays off in technology does not pay off in human relationships. His perfectionism in technology paid off. Having 30,000 round-headed rivets bored out of his airplane and replaced with flush-head rivets allowed him to break the world speed record. But his quest for the perfect woman was doomed by his self-defeating quest to impose the same paradigm of perfection upon his personal relationships. He sought the *perfect beauty* and became obsessed with Hollywood starlets and the *perfect take*. The same attention to detail he lavished on making his airplanes go faster he also devoted to the engineering of Jane Russell's bra for his movie, *The Outlaw*, where her throbbing bosom provides a frequent focus for the camera.

After twenty-six takes of one scene during the shooting of *The Outlaw*, one of his weary cohorts complained, "My God, man, you can't dissect emotion like you do an airplane. I can't break it down bit by bit. We're trying to create a mood here, and you think it's a scientific experiment. You can't attack it like an engineer." But that's what Hughes—and much of twentieth-century rationality and social engineering—have tried to do with human life.

Hughes once confessed that he wasn't all that interested in other people, that he was much more interested in "things that come out of the earth, and the way things work," i.e., *matter* and *technology*. As Hughes's decline illustrates, the materialistic will to *maximize* one's possessions, combined with an obsession for technological control, eventually leads to a minimalism that empties one's environment of all threats to perfection. At this extreme, where the essence of materialism is revealed in the ascetic's attempt at its denial, clean is never clean enough no matter how many flies his Mormons removed. Empty is never empty enough. Minimal is never minimal enough. Because "how life works" will always include some residue of original chaos, some disruption of asceticism, some perturbation of the pure forms imposed on matter. Later I'll return to the question of how and why the chaotic way life works is bound to defeat the Goal of total control. But first I want to follow Howard Hughes through his next stage of narcissistic reflection: his love/hate relationship with fame.

FAME

The death and transfiguration of Narcissus follows *the stations of recognition:* we become what we see ourselves reflected as, *and there are different levels, different stages, of reflection.*

Narcissism is all about *reflection.* First and most literally, the Narcissus myth revolves around the reflected face. But staring at oneself in the mirror gets old—especially as one's own face gets older. So, second, one sees oneself in the mirror of one's material possessions. One seeks wealth, not simply for the sake of the immediate enjoyment of one's possessions but for the sake of the more mediated pleasure of seeing one's own worth as a person reflected in one's holdings. Third, after the literal mirror, after material possessions, the mirror of public recognition in fame casts back one's reflection for all to see.

Unlike material possessions, fame is weightless. At first, fame looks like the lightest of burdens. But the loss of privacy is part of the bad news about fame. Certainly Howard Hughes suffered the paradox of a love/hate relationship with fame. Part of his affection for Katharine Hepburn lay in their shared obsession for privacy. Yet he loved the ticker-tape parade down Fifth Avenue after he broke the cross-country speed record. But he hated the invasions of his privacy by the *paparazzi*.

Is fame too high an aspiration for most of us mortals? Not at all, for there are many routes to fame, some less noble than others. Vandals and graffiti artists gain a kind of public recognition whether we like it or not. And today's media can catapult the humblest of souls to national recognition "overnight." Andy Warhol said it: these days anyone can be famous for fifteen minutes. Warhol, it was said, became famous for being famous—a lovely self-referential turn on public recognition. Of course he was an artist, and worked obsessively at producing art. But part of the Warhol phenomenon were his appearances in the media, at all the right places with all the right people. In addition to—or perhaps as part of—his art he created an *image*.

NARCISSUS IN LOVE

Following the second and third stages of narcissistic reflection —materialistic mirroring and the reflection of one's image in the mirror of fame—the evolving self comes to see itself not as a face in a mirror, not as the man who has everything, or as a bigshot, but as a subject and object of *desire*. The self comes to see that it must be recognized for more than merely what it *has*. It must be recognized for what it *is*, or what it is coming to be. And it is at this point that neither the face of the first stage, nor the image of the man-who-has-everything of the second stage, nor the public acclaim of the third stage will do. At this point a more complex, mediated reflection will be necessary for a self to see itself, and thereby become more fully what it wants to be.

Neither the clipped eyebrow nor the clipped hedge will do to improve the reflected image and thereby the reality of the postmaterialist narcissist. In the end, nothing short of love or sainthood will do. But this is just where Howard Hughes finally failed, for he was not much good at loving. He preferred adoration and control. No question that he loved women after his fashion. He could have almost any woman he wanted, and he enjoyed quite a few. He could indulge in an adoration of their beauty by shooting take after take of scenes that captured his goddesses on celluloid for all eternity. And what beauties! Not just Jane Russell, but Jean Peters, Katharine Hepburn, Jean Harlow, Ava Gardner, and the beautiful *puella*, the child starlet, Faith Domergue, whom he fell for when she was just fifteen and kept on the payroll for years without ever using in a picture.

But there is little evidence that he was particularly good at intimacy. The need for instrumental control is inconsistent with the kind of vulnerability that intimacy requires. Hughes was clearly allied with the forces of form over matter, mind over body, male over female. No partnership here. It is altogether consistent that he was attracted to little girls like Faith Domergue with whom he could play out his Pygmalion fantasies of complete control.

WE DON'T HAVE much evidence of any spiritual practice on Howard Hughes's part. But here we might be deceived. Note the uncanny similarity between the details of Hughes's terminal condition and that of some oriental holy men and mystics. He chose hermitage. He constructed his own secular monastery. He abstained from most foods and became barely more than a bag of skin and bones. He was unattached to personal possessions. He wore only the lightest and softest of clothes. He spent long hours in solitary worship of certain idols, only in place of the Buddha he contemplated his movie, *Ice Station Zebra*, which he watched some hundred and fifty times like an extended mantra. Like some of the holy men, he never cut his fingernails. His last years of life might have been very like those of the sages of old.

Of course you could dismiss Hughes as simply crazy. But then you would have to entertain the insanity of the sages. We know he took to repeating certain phrases over and over again, a recognized symptom of obsessive compulsives. But don't the sages repeat their mantras over and over again? Whether sane or crazy or both, there is no denying certain similarities between Hughes and the sages. So imagine a monologue of Howard Hughes's narcissistic reflections.

Imagine the wizened Howard Hughes mulling to himself: *Here all the while you thought you were an individual, but to your surprise you find that you are the eyes of God.*

You thought you were just an individual, but all the while your conscious mind, your individual mind, was completely unaware of all the glories and sins of the world that you were dragging along in your slipstream.

You thought you were alone, and then you discovered, when you looked into the mirror of the cosmos, that standing behind you, attached to you, forming the back of your head, as it were, were all the pain and suffering, all the brilliance, all the laws of nature, all the trivialities and contingencies that fill in the cracks of the world.

You thought you were alone, and once you stared into the mirror of the entire cosmos you saw that there behind you, there attached to you, there as part of you were all the souls that ever drew a breath and lived and died, all the living creatures large and small.

You thought you were just an individual, and once you stared into your image in the mirror of the cosmos you discovered that there is no individuality, that individuality is an illusion, a dream induced by the sleep of ordinary wakefulness.

You thought you were an individual, but then you discovered that all your thoughts were spun on a web that extends into infinity through all the words in all the languages that were ever spoken or written or sung.

You thought you were set apart, and then you discovered that every movement you make obeys all of the physical laws that every other action, every other event, obeys the very same way, and you felt the harmony that all beings share.

You thought you were an individual, but then you discovered that the boundaries of your individuality were membranes so thin, so ephemeral, that your new vision of oneness blasted them away like flying pieces of sheet metal off those planes you crashed.

You know what happens when those Mormons let the film projector stop but the lamp stays on: the image on the screen stops, then the heat of the projector lamp starts to burn the film. It starts at the center, and then the hole gets bigger as the celluloid incinerates under the heat of the lamp. Finally the screen goes all white.

That's what it's like when the boundaries of the self are burned away. A white light floods your mind and you are left gawking at the sky. But the differences return. The damn Mormons wake up, splice the film and rethread the projector. Things come into focus again. After seeing the unity of all things, all of the same old things are still there: trash and suffering, airplanes and operas, spoons and elephants. Nothing disappears, and nothing changes. But your experience of the whole, and your place in it, is different. You are connected. You are not just "you" in the way you used to understand yourself. Instead you know that your ordinary waking mind is just the growing tip of a history that includes far more than you will ever consciously remember. You know that when you touch another human being it is like one part of the whole touching another, cosmic narcissism!

When you finally wake up and see the extent of your connectedness, you will feel an immense peace. After all, how could you ever fall through this immense net when you are part of that very net. But this peace will not last, for soon you will realize that part of what this net of relationships contains is pain as well as pleasure, suffering as well as delight, and that the narrow part of the whole that resides in the body with your name can as well find itself in the pits as well as the heights. Enlightenment will not keep you from crashing if you don't fly right.

So in one sense nothing changes. The laws of nature remain the same. The rules of grammar remain the same. All the history that has ever happened remains the same. But at the same time everything is different.

You are no longer alone, despite the fact that your body will age and die independently from all other bodies. You are no longer alone, despite the fact that no one else will pay your income taxes for you. You are no longer alone, despite the fact that some of your secrets are yours alone. The day-to-day trappings of individuality will continue untouched, and your powers of vision will not burn through walls. Your biceps will not be any bigger and your memory for names will not necessarily be any better.

But once you have experienced your relatedness to all things you may become just a little more graceful. You may breathe just a little more deeply, and you may get fewer colds. Yes, there are psychosomatic effects associated with the peace that passeth all understanding, but they do not extend to leaping tall buildings at a single bound.

Narcissus never discovered these things because he looked only at his physical image. He had not yet seen his sublime image. But imagine that Howard Hughes, in his hermetic meditations, came to see these things.

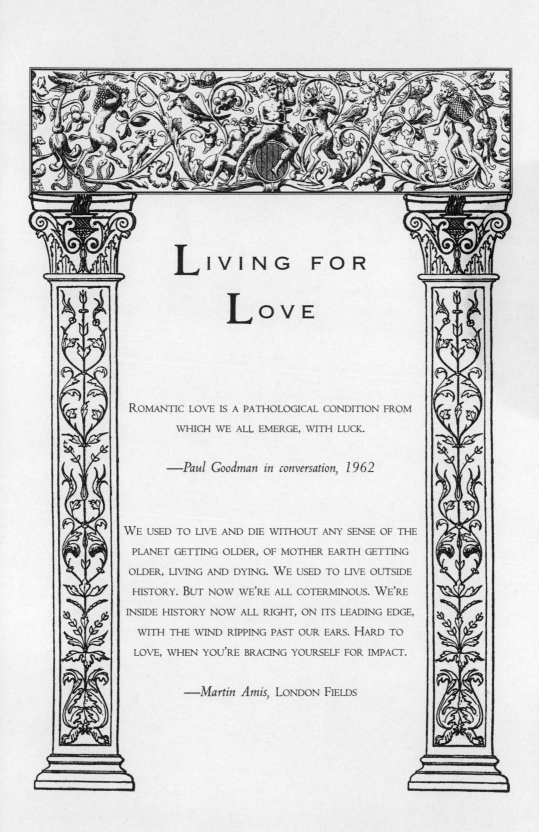

LIVING FOR LOVE

ROMANTIC LOVE IS A PATHOLOGICAL CONDITION FROM
WHICH WE ALL EMERGE, WITH LUCK.

—*Paul Goodman in conversation, 1962*

WE USED TO LIVE AND DIE WITHOUT ANY SENSE OF THE
PLANET GETTING OLDER, OF MOTHER EARTH GETTING
OLDER, LIVING AND DYING. WE USED TO LIVE OUTSIDE
HISTORY. BUT NOW WE'RE ALL COTERMINOUS. WE'RE
INSIDE HISTORY NOW ALL RIGHT, ON ITS LEADING EDGE,
WITH THE WIND RIPPING PAST OUR EARS. HARD TO
LOVE, WHEN YOU'RE BRACING YOURSELF FOR IMPACT.

—*Martin Amis,* LONDON FIELDS

6

ID HOWARD HUGHES EVER think these thoughts? Unlikely. We will never penetrate the mystery of his final years. But we do know that a twentieth-century Narcissus looking into his pool sees a reflection extending far beyond the grotto of purely private concerns: a vast network of relationships, a not very dense cloud of glistening filaments crisscrossing one another in every direction: phone calls, tax records, other people's memories, school transcripts, obligations at work, pledges of love and so on.

The postmodern narcissist will realize that he is already implicated in systems that extend beyond the immediate moment. He is always *mediated.* So his final reflection will show him that the source of his delight—or his misery—includes far more of his environment than he ever imagined. The self reflected in *the mediated sublime* is an artful creation of a life that shapes and fashions symbols as if they were reality. In a symbolic economy, symbols are as real as it gets.

By overcoming the illusion of the insular self of industrial individualism—the carefully contained *useful self*—the new self realizes that by nourishing the environment one nourishes oneself. *This* is the significance of the rich symbol of the starved body of Narcissus mulching the soil where the flower will grow. Of course one must nourish one's environment because it *is* oneself. Architects are fond of saying that people make buildings, but then buildings make people. So it is with most of culture.

But wait. Is this identification with the environment the same as the mystic's identification with the absolute? Is the evolved narcissist's death and transfiguration the same as surrendering to some preexisting divine order of things? Lila and the wispy Philip would like to think so. And so would millions of others who want to lay down the burden of selfhood and surrender to the will of God. Or the Church. Or the Revolution. Or any number of other absolute standards for the care and maintenance of the human self. But, alas, that's not "how life works."

Spike and Howard Hughes may be mistaken in their attempts to constrict their worlds down to the red dot of the isolated, narcissistic ego; but Lila and Philip will never succeed in expanding their worlds to an identification with the absolute . . . because the "absolute" is a fiction, an obsolete word like "phlogiston," signifying nothing. Just as narcissism is eventually self-defeating—as the life of Howard Hughes so clearly demonstrated—so is the attempt to find Meaning in life by identifying an absolute as one's Goal.

Lila can't rely on ideology or religion to chart her course anymore. Neither she nor Howard Hughes can find final solace in some absolute. No matter how extraordinary any single experience may be, there's always the morning after—after mystical experiences, after making love and, as even Spike has discovered, after mere sex. As a younger woman, Lila found it difficult to distinguish love from sex without hauling in some noble absolute. First the Goal of social justice and the means of revolution edified her love for Russ. Then spiritual enlightenment edified her love for Philip. With Kim she found herself wondering: *Do I really love him, or am I just looking for a warm body for sex, a partner for paying the rent, or a father for Michael?*

Lila hated second-guessing her love. Once the absolutes of politics and religion lost their hold on her life, love became more important rather than less. Now she wants True Love as her be-all and end-all. She wants True Love to substitute for all the noble causes that have crumbled over the decades. She wants love to make up for the failed Goals that inspired her path through her youth and early adulthood and the idealism that she carried westward. She wants love to heal the wounds and light the path that has become so dark with the intervening years since politics and spirituality exhausted their promise.

As Lila scales back her horizon of hope from the noble absolutes of her youth toward the more modest goal of a lasting relationship—something she has yet to achieve—she's starting to care more and more about love. There is some danger that True Love is becoming her new Goal. For Lila, romantic love has come to serve as a kind of narcissism *à deux*. Let the rest of the world take care of itself. Love will be her island of delight. In this sense, Lila's life is converging with Spike's, whose horizons are expanding beyond solitary self-absorption to include others like sweet Cindy—if only the moral pressures of love don't exhaust him.

Could love be the answer to living without a Goal? But love is so mysterious, so ineffable, and pretty hard to come by besides. Spike and Lila both face the challenge of finding the difference between sex and love. Neither knows how. Love is not an absolute. Like the self, love, too, has a history. Sex has been *cultivated* by culture, and romantic love is the result. Nature has been cultivated by different cultures, and our several histories are the result. To do what comes naturally is no longer possible for creatures who have inherited a history and a culture. We know too much. We are too civilized to mate like animals, even if we sometimes want to fuck like bunnies. So instead we talk of love, as if we knew what we were saying, and surround the chemistry of sex with the cultivation of lasting social relationships.

I feel foolish even asking the question, What *is* love? The game of defining love has gone on for centuries, from the annals of romance to this week's top forty hits. I'm not about to get it finally right in the next few pages. But we've come too far to shrink back now. So this chapter will plunge into the thicket of issues surrounding sex, love and sublimation. I'll lay out the pieces of a puzzle face up on the table, and in this and the following chapters I'll fit them together in a picture of life without a Goal.

HOW FAR HAVE we come? Some ways *back* from Lila's ambitious Goals; some ways *up* from Spike's solitary narcissism; some ways *down* from Howard Hughes's brief brush with the absolute and the peace that passeth understanding. These three paths converge on the mystery of love, which surely plays the role of The Goal for many of us. But just what are we aiming at? Lasting companionship and lust in an uneasy union? Trust, respect and friendship sealed with some form of physical magnetism? A romance so sublime that it rises above mere sex?

Each of these attempts at a definition tries to span the gulf between the physical and the sublime. From lust to much loftier sentiments; from physical magnetism to more complicated emotions; from animal sex to distinctively human structures of relationships. Both the richness and the mystery of love have something to do with this range from the lowest to the highest in human experience.

The word for describing this transformation of the lowest to the highest is sublimation. This word once meant the transformation of base material into a higher state: *the sublime.* In the ancient art of alchemy, *sublimatio* denoted the process by which the alchemist heated the philosopher's stone until it gave off sublime vapors. In later chemistry, sublimation was the name given to the direct transformation of a solid into a gas without passing through any intermediate liquid state.

Once we leave alchemy and the chemistry of gases to read poetry, philosophy and religion, the loss of a literal physical referent—gas—forces us to ask, What *is* the sublime? We need to know. For if love is central to living without a Goal, and if the mystery of love can be unlocked with a key called sublimation, then perhaps we have arrived at the right door at last, whether or not we know how to open it.

Living without a Goal *is* sublime. But sublimation is not simple. To explore its subtleties I will play on a number of themes ranging from the ancient art of alchemy, through the science of psychology, to the meaning of the information revolution. To capture the way I'll develop these themes, you could imagine this third movement as a fugue, that is, a musical construction in which the same melody repeats itself like the children's round, *"Row, row, row your boat, gently down the stream,"* and just as the first voice gets to *"Merrily, merrily,"* a second voice chimes in with the same tune all over again. The difference between Bach's fugues and children's rounds is that Bach's second voice repeats the tune five tones higher than the first. I will repeat the same melody of sublimation in different keys: the physical, the sexual, the symbolic, the economic and the ethical. As in a musical fugue, these melodies will overlap. Also like a fugue, this movement is just a little complex, so I will include some program notes to explain from time to time just what is happening and why.

Sublimation has a rich and somewhat confused history that hides secrets worth puzzling over—secrets that will be helpful to both Spike and Lila—little issues like the nature of love, the evolution of economics and the challenge of morality. In dark, mute moments of passion, three different senses of sublimation get tangled together. First, there is the delay of sexual gratification: "Shall we hump like animals and get it over with, or string it out with a little finesse?" Second, there is the span between the physical biology of sex and the meanings of the words we use in symbolic articulations of love. *Why* must Spike's dates hear the words, "I love you"? Third, the moral issue surrounding that oft-posed question: "Should we or shouldn't we?" I will untangle these three strands by dealing with sublimation as the *delay* of sexual gratification; sublimation as the *enhancement* of gratification (which will get us into something of a scandal); then I'll try to talk us out of the scandal with some language about language. In the final chapter, the coda, we'll arrive at the morality of artful living without a Goal.

LILA'S GOT A new problem with her love life. She's met a marvelous man named Ned who may be The One she was always looking for. He has a decent sense of humor and he likes her kids. But, when it comes to the physical encounter, he mixes the sheer wonder of sex with all kinds of confusing businesses. With her old Goals behind her, Lila just wants to lose herself in the flames of passion. She wants to strip naked and press flesh to flesh. But Ned has these funny ideas about erotic artistry.

Ned likes to cultivate an erotic attachment that lasts from night to day. He likes to make love with the lights on and eyes open. He doesn't like to lose himself, or Lila, in the height of passion. He likes to play. He teases. He prolongs their lovemaking with an artistry that, to Lila, seems like so much *obstruction.* He places barriers between desire and its satisfaction. He gives her lingerie, so many veils that float between their naked bodies. Why, she wonders, does he want to dress her in confections that are bound to come off sooner or later? Why doesn't he just get on with it?

Lila wants to merge in a union that knows no distinction. This, she believes, is the special gift of romantic love. She says Ned is guilty of fetishism. He says that lingerie is just one more language for articulating the enchantment of their attachment.

What is this "language of love" that Ned wants to talk? Why place intermediaries in the magnetic field of sexual attraction between their bodies?

Sublimation in one sense is the process of mediation, placing intermediaries between desire and its object, finding some romance in what would otherwise suffer the compulsiveness of instinct. And this is part of the reason sublimation is so central to living without a Goal: sublimation is the redirection of energy away from the straight shot at a target. Life can be more than a simple trajectory toward the bulls-eye of a Grand Goal. But *how* does sublimation happen? What is it that bends life's course in ways that add more in value and intensity than they detract from speed and efficiency? For, truth to tell, sublimation *does defer* some forms of gratification.

A second sense of sublimation—a second key for the melody—is symbolism. Sublimation defers life's destinations, and it does so by deviating upward toward the sublime realm of language, symbolism and the ethereal tracery of myths and images we call culture. If Goallessness as such is to be the principle of our faith, then we'll need to look much more closely at sublimation and define its link to language.

What *is* the link between sex and saying, "I love you"? If animals don't talk while they reproduce, what are they missing? According to Spike, not much. He would just as soon mate and get it over with. But that is part of Spike's self-proclaimed immaturity. He's not interested in a sustained relationship. And surely if there's one thing that love talk will get you, it's a long-term roommate at the very least. As far as Spike is concerned, better to keep quiet. The more he talks about how he's feeling, the more likely that moral scruples will keep him awake. He's getting worried about morality. And so should we. That worry will introduce the third theme of sublimation, morality and the fascination with scandal.

As in a fugue, these three themes—deferral, language and morality—will overlap one another in contrapuntal layers. This is how sublimation works: by adding layers of symbolic richness to what would otherwise sink to boring literalism.

I REMEMBER WHEN I first started thinking hard about sublimation. I had to. One evening, just after putting my children to bed, out of nowhere came the image of one of my students. She took my breath away. She used to sit in the front row. She used to come to my office to show me her poetry. Her peach-pink complexion shone in the light from the window. One day she stood by the window wearing a thin cotton shirt. A moment of silence grew immense. Desire simmered. I never touched her. Instead I began my education in sublimation. I exercised moral restraint and deferred (indefinitely and, as it happened, permanently) the gratification of my desire. And the medium for managing our way through those very intense moments was poetry. Her words moved me.

We all know that sexual pleasure is hot stuff, socially incendiary. It can wreck homes, hurt people and destroy community. No wonder sexuality is bounded within contexts sanctioned by the community: marriage and the family. To maintain stability, security and the fabric of civilization that is a condition for "higher" pleasures, the "lower" pleasures of sexual gratification must be contained, so they suffer disapproval. Children are taught discipline. "Don't touch yourself there!" The weighty edifice of repressive morality bears down upon those innocent impulses that well up from the prehistoric depths of the species. These impulses have the energy of their primitive survival value, the power of a bowstring drawn back, and this innocent energy is only confused by inhibitions. This is how the goodness of pleasure got twisted around: through the sublimation and redirection of that energy, away from its primary goal and toward some other target.

There is almost no goal-directed behavior so vehement and unbending as a mate in search of a mate. The stallion rushes straight toward the mare. Human beings engage in dances less direct. The single-minded pursuit of a goal is like a straight line connecting one's present state to one's future goal. Sublimation provides an alternative to that direct, head-on pursuit. Sublimation is curvy: it follows the course of desire rather than the compulsion of need. It redirects need's straight plunge onto a more circuitous course. But we might sometimes ask, as Lila does of Ned, why all this beating about the bush?

One answer comes down in the form of religious prohibition: thou shalt not defile the soul with the sins of the body! If your Goal is to get to heaven, go easy on the sex. You have only to pick up the papers to read about the latest scandal in the Catholic Church to see just how titanic the struggle between sexual instinct and religious repression can be. A long tradition from Plato through St. Augustine to the present preaches release from the defilements of the body. But somehow that release is hard to find. Sexual desire keeps tugging the soul back down into the body.

Another tradition reverses the polarity of values driving sexual sublimation. Oversimplifying somewhat, I'm not the first to link the impacts of Newton, Galileo, Marx, Darwin and Freud. These giants of modernity all describe the human condition as rising up out of the mud rather than descending from heaven. Matter before mind, mud before soul, sex before its sublimation into the "higher" works of art and culture. This materialist tradition offends the idealists because the materialists are not as quick to check the course of desire in the name of higher ideals. To the idealists, the materialists therefore look immoral.

Spike and Lila—and all the rest of us—are caught in the crossfire between the materialists and the idealists, a battle that has been going on for centuries. It has not ceased with the demise of communism and the so-called end of history. Quite to the contrary, the rise of modern science seemed to promise a final victory for secular materialism: no more superstitious hocus-pocus about angels and spirits now that science is on the scene. All that exists is matter and motion in space and time. So Schrödinger and his colleagues ought to be able to tell us everything we want to know about anything.

NOW LET US listen to another introduction of the theme of sublimation, this time in the key of economics. The very success of science has so transformed life that the manipulation of matter is now less important to us than processing information and defining our place in a symbol-laden world. Moving from agriculture and industry to an economy based on information and services, the transformation of everyday life amounts to nothing less than *the sublimation of the economy.* We no longer believe in angels and spirits, but the sources of our new wealth and new identities are every bit as sublime as those paragons of our old values.

Words, numbers, patents and software exist in a way quite unlike oranges, rocks, steel and hardware. The reality of words, numbers, images and reputations depends on structures of relationships rather than on their material solidity or physical characteristics. So, likewise, does the whole realm of the sublime exhibit a *different kind of existence* than physical things like rocks and oranges. The *being* of the sublime is different from the being of material things. For material things, *to be is to be an individual* with clear boundaries, an evident identity, and the ability to persist through time and space. Rocks have this kind of persistence and clear boundaries. So do oranges, until they rot; or pieces of furniture, until they are broken apart. But this grammar of existence that is so obvious for material things turns out to be dead wrong and dangerously misleading when applied to the sublime.

At stake in a proper appreciation of the sublime is nothing less than the nature of selfhood, the structuring of a satisfactory life and the meaning of wealth as we move from an economy based on solid *things* to an economy based on dematerialized information and services. None of these—services, wealth, the self—bears the label *thing* very comfortably. Services have more to do with events and experiences than with consumables or durables. Wealth is becoming less and less tangible, more and more dependent on contracts, trusts, patents and tax advantages. The self is hardly a unified *thing;* its boundaries slip off in all directions toward relationships with other people, aspirations, achievements. And finally, sex is not just the biology of animal reproduction, but the physical foundation—the

ink, the type, the pages—of the languages of love, eroticism and
romance.

IN THE INTERCONNECTIONS between the private life of the
psyche and the public world of culture and economics, some of
the moral confusion we suffer about Goals and Goallessness is
a function of a failure to keep up with the times. Our histories
and our economics are hurling us toward the sublime, but our
psychological categories—the very terms we use for feeling and
understanding our inner lives—are still stuck in the mud of
materialism and industrial utility. Freud, for one, offered a materialistic interpretation of sublimation. Plato advanced an ide-
alistic interpretation of the sublime as an absolute. Neither
approach will be adequate to Lila. And Spike? To put it in the
language of the gym that he will appreciate: he needs to learn
the isometrics of prolonged desire rather than the calisthenics
of the quickie. Sublimation will help.

There is a course between Freud and Plato toward a kind of
sublimation that can edify love above sex, but without reliance
on an absolute sublime. Relativity, the gossamer web of relationships among words in language, will be enough to make
sublimation possible. Knowledge of how language works and,
more important, how language *plays* will help to unravel the role
of sublimation in morality. But for now let's find that path
between Freud and Plato on sublimation, for that is where
Spike's and Lila's lives are converging. Without knowing it,
Spike was a Freudian and the younger Lila a Platonist. To find
the zone between artless sex and absolute love, we need to find
the path between Freud and Plato.

FREUD ON SUBLIMATION

It's hard to love while perched on a fault line between tectonic plates where the metaphysics of materialism is shearing against the symbolism of the sublime. This fault line shows up in the peculiar example of Freud's attempt to understand the process of sexual sublimation in materialistic terms. He treated the sexual juice called libido as if it obeyed the materialistic principle of constant conservation. According to Freud, as he put it in *Civilization and Its Discontents*, civilization demands the deferral of gratification, the repression of immediate instinctual drives in favor of their sublimated expression in the service of civilization.

Once real chemists took over the process of sublimation from the alchemists, they discovered that you can't get more out of less, at least not where *matter* is concerned. Vaporize any solid and the gas may fill a greater volume. But once you condense the gas and reduce the temperature to freeze it into a solid, you will have no more than you began with. Probably less due to leakage. And this was the kind of sublimation—constant conservation of mass and energy—that Freud had in mind when he described the mechanics of instinctual sublimation as a zero-sum, either/or trade-off between sex and civilization.

For all his fascination with the play of symbols in the conscious and unconscious workings of mind, Freud was, from first to last, a materialist. In his first major work, *Project for a Scientific Psychology*, he held out the hope that all the insights of psychology would ultimately be reducible to neurophysiology.

He also steadfastly refused to acknowledge *the sublime*. Just as mind is reducible to matter, so argued Freud, the products of

art and religion are reducible to processes of instinctual sublimation. The higher mysteries of art and religion are just so
many shadows cast on the clouds by the earthbound drama of
instinctual energies. Sex is real. Art and religion are works of
illusion. So speaks the materialist. So speaks the reductionist
with phrases like "Art is *nothing but* the sublimation of sexual
energy." So, finally, speaks the cynic to whom "It's all the
same"—just a series of rearrangements of the same old matter.
You can't get more out of less.

Freud favored immediate instinctual gratification. He
thought that civilized sublimation was generally a bad bargain.
To hear him tell the tale of the civilizing process, we invented
morality and religion to keep from fucking ourselves blind and
useless—in a well-worn phrase, to *delay gratification.* We redirected our sexual energy away from the immediate goal of sexual gratification into the medium of culture: cathedrals, music,
works of art. But the substitutes for immediate gratification,
according to Freud, may not be as good as the original Goal.
Once sexual energy is redirected toward other goals, the process
of sublimation, according to Freud, works like leaky plumbing:
it loses much of its juice somewhere along the way.

Civilization's demands may turn out to be greater than the
rewards of gratification deferred; hence the discontents. According to Freud, the deviation of desire away from its sexual
goal ends up detracting more than it could ever add to desire's
final gratification. "If civilization requires such sacrifices, not
only of sexuality but also of the aggressive tendencies in mankind, we can better understand why it should be so hard for
man to feel happy in it. In actual fact, primitive man was better
off in this respect, for he knew nothing of any restrictions on

his instincts. As a set-off against this, his prospects of enjoying his happiness for any length of time were very slight. Civilized man has exchanged some part of his chances of happiness for a measure of security."

For Freud, the hydraulics of sublimation can be no better than a zero-sum game: *either* you spend your energy in the immediate gratification of sexual instinct, *or* you redirect all that seething libido toward more civilized goals like art, religion and the rest of what we call culture. And there is only so much libido to go around. "Since a man does not have unlimited quantities of psychical energy at his disposal, he has to accomplish his tasks by making an expedient distribution of his libido. What he employs for cultural aims he to a great extent withdraws from women and sexual life." *This* is the deep background behind such oft-repeated sentences as "Sorry, dear, I have to go to the office."

These days we aren't quite so quick to set up the drama in the sexist way that Freud did. "Women represent the interests of the family and of sexual life. The work of civilization has become increasingly the business of men, it confronts them with ever more difficult tasks and compels them to carry out instinctual sublimations of which women are little capable." Look out, Sigmund: listen to the sound of righteously outraged feminist hoofbeats in the distance.

Now that we've discovered that women *are* capable of the deferral of gratification it takes to get through law school, we no longer countenance the notion that civilization is only a man's game. Now women, too, can suffer the discontents that Freud described. The drama of sublimation doesn't pit man against woman for the sake of civilization. The drama pits immediate gratification against deferred, sublimated gratification, and either gender can choose either part. *She* may be the one to suit up and leave *him* at home.

But if this is all feminism has achieved—a more even distribution of civilized discontents among men and women alike—then we haven't gained much. We can do better. Freud was wrong about more than the casting for this drama of sublimation. He was mistaken in his choice of metaphor: plumbing. This metaphor led to the mechanistic, materialistic law of *the constant conservation of libido.*

Carried over into the psychology of sublimation, the materialistic principle of the conservation of matter and energy leads straight into the idea that life is all about pushing instinctual energy around from one goal to another. If all the results are reducible to rearrangements of the same basic stuff, then what's the point? You can never get more out of less.

SUBLIMATION IS THE detour that redirects the straight and headlong lunge for instinct's goal. If a human life is more like a dance than a lurch toward a single goal, then the choreography of sublimation should interest those who make Goallessness the principle of their faith. But if sublimation is the alternative to racing straight toward a goal, we've got to come up with a better version of sublimation than the one we get from Freud. We've got to come up with something more appealing than the reshuffling of the same old stuff.

I do not see sublimation as hydraulic redirection with probable reduction due to leakage in the psychic plumbing. Libido is not like Prestone antifreeze. There is no Newtonian law for the constant conservation of libido. Through sublimation, we *can* get more out of less. We can fantasize our sex and have it too. The symbolic does not detract from the so-called real. To the contrary, the brain can be the consummate erogenous zone.

Sublimation is not a zero-sum game. The sublime is not just a consolation prize given to the instincts after repressive civilization defers the sexual sweepstakes. But in coming up with a better story about sublimation we run the risk of reverting to a premodern approach to the sublime. What would such an approach look like, and why is it as inadequate as Freud's?

THE PLATONIC SUBLIME

Contrary to Freud, Platonism treats the sublime as if it were there waiting for us as we struggle upward from material reality. The sublime would include all those experiences of enlightenment that Freud reduces to sublimations of libido. But, for the Platonist, the sublime is not only irreducible, it is somehow *more* real than the material steps that lead toward it.

What are some examples of this always already beckoning sublime? Heaven, for one. Or the kind of bliss in this life described in the oriental literature of enlightenment. Or, to retreat from the mystical and spiritual to a more secular philosophy, take Plato's realm of ideas: pure forms without material content; values, norms and standards of perfection. In Plato's philosophy, these were described as *more real* than those tangible things we think of as real, but which turn out to be pale imitations of their more perfect versions in the realm of ideas.

Plato opposed these eternal ideas to a lower realm of material things. Eternal ideas have *being;* temporal things are mired in mere *becoming.* This chain of oppositions—eternal to temporal, being to becoming, ideal to material—is a secular version of a religious order that would put heaven over hell, God over man, and soul over body.

The Goal for those starting at the bottom of this Platonic hierarchy is to scale the great chain of being from the veil of illusion in the physical world to the clarity of vision available in the eternal order of the sublime. There, in the Platonic realm of pure ideas, time gives way to eternity and the pain and suffering of becoming will be banished by the bliss of pure being. Sounds like a consummation devoutly to be wished, this Platonic version of the sublime. Or does it? Not to Nietzsche.

"What kind of man reflects in this way? An unproductive, suffering kind, a kind weary of life. If we imagine the opposite kind of man, he would not need to believe in what has Being. More, he would despise it as dead, tedious, indifferent." Nietzsche, the proponent of Goallessness as such, sees how the Goal of sublime being works as a lure for those who are sick of becoming, who cannot tolerate *real time*, who want to stop the world and escape to a place where nothing happens—no planes, no trains, no pain or suffering. Sounds like a Club Med for long-dead mummies.

Of course this is a caricature of the Platonic sublime, but perhaps *becoming* isn't all that bad. Perhaps the reading of sublimation that looks upward toward an already posited sublime is no better than a reductionism that looks downward toward base instincts redirected through sublimation. Perhaps both readings amount to opposite ways of escaping real time.

MY EXPERIENCE TELLS me that much of what I have read in texts from Plato to Freud is wrong. And more important than the texts themselves, what we've inherited from the Western European culture that embraced those texts is deeply confusing. The contest between pleasure and repression has been miscast. The split between body and mind, and its correlation with the contest between instinctual energy and civilization, derives from a past when the furniture of life was different from what it is today. Back when we spent less time shuffling symbols and more time using our muscles, the furniture of our universe was almost entirely physical. Now, however, we live in a world largely composed of symbols, or things that are not *just* things but, like the flowers in a gift bouquet, things that have now gained symbolic meaning in addition to their sheer physicality.

Both the Freudian and the Platonic readings of sublimation end up embracing what is "dead, tedious, indifferent." For Plato, the process of sublimation is subordinate to its *goal:* the sublime. For Freud, the process is derivative from its materialistically conceived *origin,* the libidinal energy that gets sublimated. In neither case is the process of sublimation appreciated in its own right—as an artful and creative bootstrapping operation that generates more out of less.

For Freud, the emblematic experience of sublimation might be the cold shower: a less than pleasurable means for redirecting libidinal energy from where it wants to go. For Plato, the emblematic experience of sublimation is an abstinence that avoids sex altogether—the relationship that is "purely Platonic." Neither reading of sublimation helps us see how life can have the sublimity of a Sunday drive to nowhere, how getting there can be more than half the fun. Neither the materialist nor the idealist reading of sublimation allows us to see how delaying gratification can actually *enhance* gratification rather than diminishing it. Freud's version of sublimation is second best to simple sexual gratification; at worst, a nihilistic reshuffling of libido signifying nothing—a meaningless redirection of energy.

Plato's version of the sublime offers too much where Freud offers too little. For Spike to delay gratification and Lila to take delight in Ned's gifts, what's needed is a version of sublimation that offers more than Freud's cold shower and less than Plato's ascetic communing with a completely dematerialized sublime. Sticking for a moment with the sexual medium for sublimation, we need to identify emblematic experiences of sexuality that lie between the Freudian and Platonic extremes. I can think of two. First, Tantric yoga; second, with Ned's help, lace.

Tantra and
Lace

It is not the artistic aptitudes that are
secondary sexual characters as some shams and
shamans have said. It is the other way around:
sex is but the ancilla of art.

—*Vladimir Nabokov*

7

ANTRIC YOGA IS AN ORIENTAL practice that arouses sexual desire but stops short of the release of excitement in orgasm. Tantric priestesses are expert at exciting erotic energy, and expert also at ceasing from their ritualized ministrations just short of the final moment. Tantric yoga has a long history that has spawned whole traditions of erotic art that would be regarded as scandalous by Western Christians. Tantrism is based on a cultivation of erotic energy, a refinement of eros toward something more sublime, a sublimation that is not reducible to base instincts. Nor is Tantric practice particularly goal-directed. The goal of orgasm is deferred indefinitely; but the sexless preoccupation with the Platonic sublime is abandoned with the first move of the priestess.

Resolutely Western, Ned takes his culture with a spoon rather than chopsticks, so the closest he'll come to Tantrism is lace. Neither opaque nor transparent, lingerie conceals as it reveals, and reveals as it conceals. And of course—this is the whole point—as the goal hidden behind a veil, a body clad in lace can be more alluring than one completely naked.

Lace defers the goal of total revelation; it demands a detour around its artful contrivance. The excitement that lace induces will be higher, not lower, than immediate, unmediated gratification. Lace is a medium that adds to eros by stimulating the mind rather than subtracting from eros as if it were some liquid matter that could be lost down the drain. Lace incites lust by offering just enough to provoke an active imagination, but not so much that too little is left to the imagination.

It takes a mind to appreciate the shimmering significance of lingerie. It's doubtful that lace has much effect on dogs or horses. Granted, the animal kingdom has its plumage and its mating dances. But I doubt that quite so much excitement can be generated among animals by a play of associations that involves memories, customs, inhibitions, the whole drama of courtship that culture creates. This work of culture, this cultivation of an otherwise raw and animal instinctual energy, requires mind.

Consider the mental associations involved in the symbolism of different colors of lace. White lace for the bride's wedding gown is innocent—almost. It is not as innocent as plain white fabric. When worn as frills, white lace might be innocent. But when worn as a covering for whatever is then manifestly less than covered, white lace is hardly innocent. But the bride is meant to be supremely seductive in her innocence.

Black lace connotes the art of seduction: hints of erotic

delights beyond one's eager imagination. Pink lace is part of the world of little girls—and not so little girls. Just as red roses convey a message that is altogether different from the message of white roses, so does red lingerie differ from white as hot differs from cool. The symbolism of lace is every bit as complex and fully articulated as the symbolism of flowers. Both are redolent of romance. Both are dependent on a certain superfluity. Like the petals of an orchid, the frills on a pair of panties express a spirit of extravagance, a flaunting of mere functionality.

Some fool will surely try to exploit this analogy between lace and flowers to argue the biological functionality of lingerie, as if lace were simply the evolutionary successor of flower petals and peacock feathers. What is the *use value* of lace? Utilitarian answer: seduction, mating and the propagation of the species. But the biology of stimulus and response obeys laws altogether different from the grammar of significance. For a symbol to be sexually significant, mental associations must be made. It is not simply a matter of chemistry, even in the case of flowers.

In past centuries a poet might have waxed eloquent about the physical qualities of flowers: their color, their aroma, the shapes of their petals. Now we take for granted the botany and biology of flowers; it is their *meaning* that matters. A good florist can make a big difference to how others understand you. Your florist is your agent in communicating certain kinds of messages. How do flowers function as signs or symbols? How is it that red roses differ from white roses in more ways than mere color?

The meaning of red roses has very little to do with weights or volumes or trajectories or the cause-effect logic of mechanical pushes and pulls. Schrödinger's wave equation won't help you calculate your date's interpretation of the meaning of a bouquet. Meaning derives from systems of relationships, from semantics and grammar and syntax. These structures of relationships have a completely different way of *being*, a different order of existence with completely different metrics. You would not say a physical entity was *profound*, nor could you describe an idea as *ovoid*. Words are not cogs in machines. Symbols don't do their work the same way levers and cranks and pulleys do.

We all recognize these differences in ways of *being* when we focus on them consciously. But it's easy to miss the significance of the difference when unconscious habits borrowed from centuries of physical manipulations drift over into the ways we push symbols around. No one reaches for a hacksaw to cut a budget. And no one would imagine that reasoning alone could build a building. But flying on the wings of metaphor—language's use of likenesses—we often import the logic of physical processes into our mental manipulations, as Freud did in treating libido materialistically. Spike and his friends with their language peppered with "likes" are right about one thing: almost nothing in the postmodern world *is* only what it is. Almost everything is what it is and *like* something else besides, symbolically speaking. Anything can tell a tale including a lot more than meets the eye.

Our sex lives are surely built on a solid base of purely physical biology. But what we then do with the physical mechanics of sex varies so wildly from culture to culture, and from person to person, that any attempt to reduce that extravagant diversity to a single law of physical stimulus and response is patently absurd. A certain scalloped curve across a certain shape of flesh can evoke a very specific response with amazing regularity. But this reduction of seduction to the mechanics of stimulus and response misses the entire point. It confuses the erotic with the obscene.

The erotic articulates desire in many languages. The obscene reduces desire to dumbness. The erotic draws on the riches of the symbolic dimension. The obscene silences the symbolic with the blare of literalism. Erotic delight is a kind of play that wants to go on forever. Obscenity always ends up looking like work, an effort to get it over with. Obscenity, very simply, is too goal-directed. The erotic makes room for the superfluous, time for delight, and space for symbolic significance that is more like play than the workings of stimulus-response reactions.

THE USE AND ABUSE OF UTILITY

What is the utility of flowers? You can just hear Farmer Brown in his overalls complaining to his long-suffering wife in calico, "What's the point? What's the purpose? What's the goal?" If you were going to grow a crop, make it edible. Likewise one could ask about the use value of lace. One might as well ask, What is the utility of laughter? What is the use value of life? What is the value of *use* value?

Taking art and aesthetic judgment as the paradigm for composing a life, we would do well to question the usefulness of *utility* as the measure of value. Utilitarianism is the morality of industrialists. By basing morality on quantitative calculations of the greatest good for the greatest number, utilitarians leave morality up to the engineers. But can we submit to the engineering of humanity without surrendering the very humanity we would engineer? The tedious calculations of the utilitarians will tell us nothing we want to know about the language of lace. Nor will the calculations of the utilitarians tell us what we now want to know about politics or economics or morality. The sublimation of the economy from the solidity of industrial goods to the ephemerality of information and services leaves us in a world where the old vocabulary of durable goods with marginal *utility* gives way to a new vocabulary of evanescent experiences of marginal *intensity*.

But intensity is very much in the eye of the beholder, more so than utility, which, presumably, could be objectively calculated. The economics of the sublime puts the consumer in the driver's seat of the economy because differences among consumers' tastes determine the quality of their experiences more than opinions determine the utility of a truckload of steel. A ton of steel is a ton of steel is a ton of steel. But a rose is *not just* a rose. Nor is one person's taste in lingerie necessarily like another's, as Lila and Ned have discovered. And how foolish it would be to dismiss these differences, as Farmer Brown dismisses the utility of flowers, for lingerie's failure to function as protective apparel. Lace is not supposed to keep out the rain.

THE SCANDAL OF GOALLESSNESS

All very well and good, you say. *We may be moving from an economics of need to an economics of desire, from the realm of physical necessities to the realm of sublime freedom, from the oom-pah-pah of the industrial march to a more lyrical postmodern melody. But what about morality? How do we navigate once the absolutes are gone? What are our political goals? Let them eat lace?*

Morals are at stake in the delights of lingerie, not only in the naughtiness of its consumption but also in the political economics of its production. There was a time when the working conditions for the manufacture of lace were as dirty a secret to society as the lace that was hidden beneath yards of Victorian clothing. Among the most moving passages in Marx's works are his descriptions of the lace factories scattered across nineteenth century England. These hovels of servitude and oppression had been observed and painstakingly described in the reports of the Children's Employment Commission published every year between 1863 and 1867, just when Marx was reading his way through the British Museum Library and writing the first volume of *Das Kapital.*

"It is not at all uncommon in Nottingham," Marx quotes from the Children's Commission Reports, "to find 14 to 20 children huddled together in a small room, of, perhaps, not more than 12 feet square, and employed for 15 hours out of the 24, at work that of itself is exhausting, from its weariness and monotony, and is besides carried on under every possible unwholesome condition. . . . Even the very youngest children work with a strained attention and a rapidity that is astonishing, hardly ever giving their fingers rest or slowing their motion. If a question be asked them, they never raise their eyes from their work from fear of losing a single moment."

The teeth-grinding poignancy of the reports from the factory inspectors on the working conditions in the lace industry comes from the contrast between the luxuriousness of lace and the wretched oppression of the workers who made it. Of course lace today is made by machines. It is not woven by children huddled in dim gaslight. (But what about all that silk that says "Made in China"? One hears stories of factories employing slave labor in the western provinces. . . .)

Is it not scandalous to fix upon the luxuriousness of lace as a paradigm for the new economy when millions still lack the barest of necessities? To which, of course, the answer is, *Yes, it is scandalous.* Rather than shrinking back from scandal, however, let us inspect the anatomy of scandal: it fascinates all the more, the more it repels. This is its magic: in shocking our sense of propriety, scandal widens the horizons of desire and liberates us from the commonplace. New things become possible, but how shocking! And therefore how much *more* desirable! And so the cycle goes round in a feedback loop that soon sets telephones buzzing with rumors of a new scandal: *Somebody got over the wall of propriety*—as I got over the wall out of Exeter. But is this freedom from the strait and narrow won only at the price of transgression?

WHAT IS THE source of our fascination with sin? To conscious beings who have been reared in a culture that cultivates inhibitions, the fascination goes beyond the direct appeal of physical pleasure. There is a special lure to what is naughty, for the very fact that it has been labeled as naughty. I felt the fascination of outlaw country while seated behind the wheel of my Mercury. Later I was lured by the guilty pleasures of pinball. The Living Theater's nudity in *Apocalypse Now* played to packed houses of people drawn by the transgression of propriety. Call this dynamic perverse if you like, but until we appreciate the logic of temptation we will not be able to withstand its lure.

Utilitarianism lacks the subtlety we need to grasp the oscillations of temptation. Utilitarianism springs from an attitude that sees everything in terms of an overly simplistic means/ends mentality. Utilitarianism sees every action as a more or less successful means toward some end, a tool toward some goal. To enter into battle with utilitarianism on its own turf—the calculation of better and worse *means*—is to lose the war against an instrumental approach to ethics.

In the absence of absolutes, we may not always know *why* certain acts are wrong even if we know *that* they are wrong. At the center of everyday life we know that it is wrong to lie, cheat, steal or inflict cruelty. We no longer say these transgressions are wrong because they are sins that displease God or because they violate some equally absolute set of standards transcending all cultural differences. Why, then, are they wrong? Because they violate some utilitarian calculus for computing the greatest happiness for the greatest number? Is that the goal of morality? To *maximize* the sum total of happiness? I think Nietzsche nailed the basic assumption of utilitarianism when he quipped, "Man does not seek after happiness; only the Englishman does that."

I want to suggest a different tack, one that, like utilitarianism, would preserve morality without absolutes, but one that relies more on art than on mathematics for its metaphors. Aesthetic judgment in the symbolic order provides better models for moral reasoning than the mathematics and physics of the physical order.

We do not *calculate* our way through moral crises . . . unless we have been infected with utilitarian philosophy. Those who are innocent of both absolutes and utilitarian rationality tend to *intuit* their way toward the good much in the same way as they make judgments about the beautiful. Morality, like the appreciation of beauty, is less a matter of *maximizing* than of *savoring:* seeing patterns, sensing coherence, delighting in what *fits,* feeling the appropriateness of the singular part to the complex whole.

Simplistic codes of ethics divide the world too neatly into good and evil. Whether it is Reagan drawing a line around Russia as "the evil empire," or religious commandments with their "Thou shalt nots," or the rule book at Exeter with its lists of punishable offenses, simple codes ignore the mysterious kinship of saints and sinners, and the oft-noted closeness of the highest and the lowest. Such simple codes seem to ignore the kinship between *freedom* and *transgression.*

If all the world were as simple as childhood games, and the difference between right and wrong as easy to see as a foot that is in bounds or out of bounds, then growing good human beings would be as easy as growing good asparagus. It would be a scientific issue: how to maximize certain outputs for certain inputs. But we human beings are far more complex than asparagus, not least because we speak and live a large part of our lives in the realm of the symbolic sublime where boundaries are none too clear.

With the best of intentions, we tend to misconstrue the structure of right and wrong in a world filled with symbols. Hoping for the clarity and literalism to be found in the physical order, where sheep can be clearly distinguished from goats and gold clearly separated from silver, we imagine that good and evil can be kept apart with equal clarity. But the symbolic order is rife with ambiguity and, unlike the realm of physical necessity, riddled with arbitrariness and rent by differences of mere taste.

Lace may be naughty stuff. Not only in the Tantric teasing involved in its use but also in the political economics of its production, lace carries a legacy of associations that flirt with evil. No wonder Marx was moved to expropriate the expropriators. The oppression of children is a social obscenity. Marx cannot be faulted for wanting to rid the earth of that obscenity. But the social experiment called Marxism on the left, like fascism on the right, runs the danger of dividing the world too neatly—too materialistically—between the forces of good and the forces of evil.

By focusing on dramatic extremes of obvious evil, Marx missed the duplicity and ambiguity essential to most moral predicaments. By making morality look simpler than it is, Marx begat Marxism, a political strategy with a clear Goal: revolution as the means toward the end of a classless society. But the Goal of a classless society did not come to pass as planned. The grand political strategies that provide Goals for their partisans —whether the final solution of the fascists or the classless society of the Marxists—produce more evil in the end than they set out to eradicate.

Grand Goals have a nasty way of turning sour. By insisting on seeing people as fully naked or fully clothed in the mantle of goodness, utopian politics of both the left and the right hold up the Goal of moral purity and complete innocence. By separating the world into unambiguous black and white, political crusaders miss the shades of gray that color everyday life. They miss the duplicity inherent in the structure of evil.

The next chapter offers an account of the duplicity (rather than obvious clarity) of evil by grounding it in the very nature of language and its potential for ambiguity. Unless we grasp both the good news and the bad news about sublimation, then we are likely to fall back into a kind of latter-day Platonism with the sublime as our Goal. Lots of people do it: they become zealots of one fundamentalism or another. Not just the radical Muslims, but eco-feminists, struggling alcoholics and born-again Christians live by a rule book. Unlike artists, they have no taste for transgression or, consequently, for freedom. They know precisely where the goal line is, and their whole lives are aimed toward crossing it. But the rest of us know that life is not so simple. We just don't know exactly how it got so complex.

Most of us hover somewhere between the extremes of good and evil. We let in just enough knowledge to make us feel slightly guilty about our relatively good fortune, but not enough to make us sacrifice the fruits of that fortune. We don't all imitate Albert Schweitzer or follow Florence Nightingale. Nor do we harden our hearts on purpose or aspire to be like Uncle Scrooge before his transformation. We simply meander as best we can toward a third path between the extremes of sainthood and callous oblivion.

In tacking back and forth between Spike's narcissism and Philip's mysticism, we end up neither satisfied with solitude nor convinced by the Grand Goals that would motivate crusades to save the world. But moral dilemmas remain on the path between lofty solitude and the comforts of conformity to socially prescribed absolutes.

Goody-goody ethics are no good: they give you no sense of the way through hell. They ignore the lessons of Dante, or of Orpheus. They do not enable you to navigate the underworld. It is not The Good that we need to know to get along, but how to recognize the deceptive and duplicitous face of evil. No ethics I know helps you live well with the inevitability of imperfection. Not how to perfect one's music but how to live after making a mistake—that is the question. How can one look oneself in the mirror after a nasty divorce, a bad business deal, a betrayal of confidence? How to live with an irremediable scar across your memory, and how to forgive yourself for your carelessness when, after all, you could have helped it?

We've left the religious/agricultural era when life was fairly simple: hunger the enemy, salvation the Goal, and God in His heaven to serve as creator and umpire for the human game. We're just now leaving the political/industrial era in which ideology replaced belief and materialism replaced a reverence for the sublime. We may suspect that the Grand Goals provided by religion and politics are no longer appropriate as navigational aids in this new era of information and economics. But we still insist on finding other Goals to give our lives meaning and a sense of purpose.

We might like to replace salvation and revolution with other Goals of equal grandeur rather than accept Goallessness as such as the principle of our faith. Centuries of sublimation have taught us to live our lives and shape our selves as *means* to transcendent *ends,* so we find it difficult to imagine a life or a self that is not shaped and defined in terms of Grand Goals. And I suspect that it is not quite enough to invoke the virtues of modesty. It is not psychologically satisfying to say, "Think small. Scale back your aspirations." Ambition is not a sin. Individuals must still be able to dream. But how, then, to determine the *best* course of action once the Grand Goals of religion and ideology have been recognized as perverse?

What is the meaning of "best" once all absolutes have been abandoned? Can there be any rationale for preferring one goal over another? Once we abandon the old absolutes, there's a danger of sliding down a slippery slope into the slough of hedonism and subjective relativism: settling for whatever feels good at the time.

The next chapter seeks a foothold on that slippery slope between the old absolutes and abject relativism. If the absolutes are gone, can politics take their place as a means for providing meaning and noble Goals? A brief look at recent history suggests that Fukuyama is partly right. Ideologies *are* as obsolete as absolutes. So we will need to scale back the scope of meaning from grand political strategies with their ideological Goals to a more modest morality that is tactical and aesthetic rather than strategic and ideological.

Shades of
Gray

The Good that we would we do not, and the
evil that we would not we do.

—*Romans 7:19*

8

VEN AS WE REDUCE THE SCALE
of our concerns from the ideological to
the moral, we will find ourselves slipping
on signs and symbols that are more am-
biguous than national borders. As with the different sources of
self-esteem among cattlemen in Texas and agents in Hollywood, so here the solidity of the medium will make a difference
once again. In place of the relatively clear borders that used to
define political issues, moral issues turn on signs and symbols
whose meaning and significance are less determinate than
mountain ranges or coastlines. The first half of this chapter
plays in the moral register, exploring some ironies and ambiguities that plague politics and ethics these days. The second half
of the chapter will add a line from the symbolic register to

address the difference between *physical* boundaries and *symbolic* ambiguities, and its importance for living without a Goal. But first we want to see just what has happened: what's gone wrong with the Grand Goals defined by political ideologies?

THE POLITICS OF IRONY

Democracy is in trouble when voters don't achieve the goals they had in mind when they voted. Over the past several decades a disturbing pattern has emerged: only conservative administrations can get away with liberalizing measures, while left-wing administrations are forced to turn conservative. A first example: it took Republican Richard Nixon to reopen relations between the United States and China. A Democrat would have been accused of consorting with the communists. Second, Lyndon Johnson was elected with the goal of getting America out of Vietnam and he sank the nation deeper into the quagmire. A third political irony: the verdict on Johnson's war on poverty seems mixed at best. While some of the poor have benefited from education and welfare programs, many have become trapped in pockets of self-reproducing poverty. Well-intentioned programs in rent control reduce incentives for building or maintaining low-income housing, so more people end up on the streets. Fourth and final in this list of perverse effects of political manipulation: a Rand study on the results of the war against drugs shows that the ultimate outcome of DEA activity was to raise the profit margin on cocaine, increase the incentives for dealers and thereby increase rather than decrease the traffic in crack.

If a step toward a goal leads to two steps away from that same goal, and a step to the left leads to two steps to the right, then voters find themselves confused by the Minsk-Pinsk syndrome. According to an old Yiddish tale, one salesman asks another, "Are you traveling to Minsk or to Pinsk?" When the second salesman says, "To Minsk," the first replies, "You liar, you really are going to Minsk."

When distrust runs so deep that expressions of intention are taken to be veiled intimations to the contrary, then rational strategy becomes nearly impossible. The setting and gaining of national goals seems fruitless. When hawks beget doves and doves beget hawks; when policies like rent control end up producing higher rents; when conservatives are the only ones who can liberalize, and liberals have to turn conservative, then policy makers enter a hall of mirrors from which there seems to be no simple escape.

No wonder the young seem lacking in political idealism! The recent lessons of history have been hard on innocent good will. Once the Minsk-Pinsk syndrome creates a politics of irony, then obviousness becomes obsolete. The direct pursuit of political goals seems more likely to produce unintended side effects at best, or the opposite of the intended goals at worst. Deviousness then becomes the antidote to naïveté. Even François Mitterand, after starting his term as an avowed socialist, was forced to admit, "In no way am I the enemy of profit, if it's apportioned fairly. Yes, you can make a fortune here [in France]." Lacking faith in the efficacy of political solutions, smart people turn to wealth creation in the marketplace as a means of improving the human lot, starting with their own backyards.

TACTICAL ETHICS

Tactical ethics focuses on particulars, on what is very close at hand, on the human scale of everyday life, on the texture of contingencies that determine the shape and feel of a morally ambiguous situation. A finer grain of analysis is required when you trade morality-by-commandment for morality-by-judgment. With a morality based on absolute commandments, one that always steers by a carefully determined set of fixed strategies, the general features of a situation permit one to make appropriate classifications for any necessary moral determinations. *No abortions allowed! Pregnant and unmarried with three other children under five? We don't even want to know about the other children. They are irrelevant to the commandment: no abortions allowed.*

A tactical ethics based on judgment rather than commandment would not automatically conclude that an abortion is appropriate in any given case. It would not *automatically* conclude anything at all, for morality is not computation. The postmodern moralist would enter the anguish of the situation, feel all of its variables, look as far and wide as possible for innocent bystanders and errant responsibilities, then reach a judgment on that unique situation considered in the context of as much of the universe as pregnant parents could possibly comprehend.

Advising young lovers to "be good" is not likely to succeed if the suggestion is to pursue chastity at the price of pleasure. What is our incentive for "being good"? Surely not the Goal of salvation. Most of us suspect that when our life is done we will burn in the crematorium or rot in the ground. We will neither sprout wings and fly to heaven nor sizzle for eternity in the fires of hell. Most grownups know that their punishments and rewards will come here on this earth in this lifetime or not at all.

The carrots and sticks of religion no longer motivate mature adults in postmodern times. Even Catholics use contraceptives. And the ego ideals being internalized from the mythologies of postmodern culture are not likely to lead to "good" behavior. Today's ideal egos are hardly pillars of the community. Our heroes look more like Mickey Rourke than John Wayne. We have seen the apocalypse in Cinemascope with Dolby sound, we have felt the fear of being mugged in our major cities, and we lack faith in guarantees of progress toward a happy ending for our trials. These days we know we need guides through hell, updated versions of Dante's *Inferno*.

All is *not* permitted. Not the pollution of the environment, not the descent into hopeless hedonism. But how are we to pick our way between Lila's absent Absolutes that would tell us *precisely* what *is* permitted and Spike's arbitrary nihilism that permits anything and everything?

Without a master narrative of an overarching religion shared by all nations and cultures, we lack the unifying culture that would provide a common ground for a shared morality. Lacking the common thread of practices that allow the participants in different histories to communicate with one another, people are hard pressed to find a common set of rules and understandings for their exchanges with one another. Regulation of trade becomes difficult because the same word has different meanings in different cultural contexts. The sharing of tips that would be condemned as "insider trading" in New York might be the normal practice of helping your friends in Tokyo or Hong Kong. "Nepotism" in one culture reflects predominant family values in another.

Morally vacant relativism is the dark edge of pluralism. But it is not inescapable and does not have to become the pernicious alternative to the old absolutes. There are ways to defend values that transcend the individual without depending on universal, absolute commandments covering everyone everywhere always. Recall from the discussion of the obsolescence of the absolute that the five forms of relativity that replaced faith in their respective absolutes did *not* hurl each discipline into incoherence: the international economy still works without a gold standard. "Baskets" of currencies act as ballast to stabilize the sloshing back and forth of relative exchange rates among different currencies. Might there be baskets of morals that outweigh the impulses of the moment without depending on the "gold standard" of absolute commandments?

Navigation is possible despite Einstein's relativization of absolute space. Relativity theory doesn't alter the usefulness of road maps. In the realm of human-scale itineraries, a mile is still a mile. The relativization of space distorts the metric only for much longer journeys measured in light-years. A similar argument can be made in the realm of ethics. The customs of a community or a tradition may be sufficient for dealing with most moral crises *within* that community. The relativization of values takes its toll only when we attempt to span vast cultural distances, as in Salman Rushdie's daring literary travels between Islam and the West.

Language still works despite the lack of simple reference to some absolute reality. The latticework of each language is sufficient for the French, the Germans, the Americans and the Japanese, etc. Might there be as many grammars of morals, similar but not identical, that are sufficient for the moral needs of individuals within each culture? We get into trouble trying to find foundations for our values only when we insist on digging deeper through the loam of our own particular culture in search of the absolute bedrock beneath all linguistic and cultural differences.

There is an oft-repeated story about Indian cosmology. A fakir tries to persuade a Westerner that the world rests on the back of an elephant who is in turn standing on the back of a giant turtle. In the way of an inquiring Westerner, the question naturally arises: "On what is the turtle standing?" To which the fakir answers, "Ah, sahib, after that it's turtles all the way down!"

In our relativistic, postmodern world mediated by veils of ambiguity, it's interpretations all the way down. The gap opened up by the interpretability of signs forever separates our symbols from a rigorous, one-to-one foundation in physical reality. And even if we could ground our symbols in that reality, our understanding of matter is no longer as deterministic as it once was. Both below us in what used to feel like a physical fundament, and above us where we used to imagine some religious or Platonic blueprint in the sky, we now sense uncertainty and ambiguity.

Chaos theory becomes instructive at just this point where the mechanically minded perfectionist wishes to impose form on the geologic fundament of recalcitrant matter. Once upon a time science seemed to suggest that there might be a hope of taming matter. With a few more discoveries and a lot of hard work we could get below the level of mere probabilities to measure and predict those certainties that surely lay like bedrock at the base of all existence. As surely as solid bottom could be found beneath every wave of liquid ocean—if only we plumbed deep enough—just as surely there should be a determinate hard edge to reality beneath every cloud of mere probability.

Now the sciences do not testify so certainly about certainty. The tide of determinism is turning. The understanding of probabilities in nature no longer attributes the gap between certainty and probability to human ignorance of true causes that must be operating deterministically whether we have identified and measured them or not. Now we understand matter to be irreducibly probabilistic. The very best descriptions we can give for subatomic "particles" are statistical probability distributions: equations that say, in effect, the chances of locating "particle a" at point x are such and such. "Particle a"—and the quotation marks are crucial—begins to look more like a wave than a solid, hard-edged entity. Unlike the ocean that has a solid floor, even physical reality may be waves all the way down.

The very concept of matter has been dematerialized if, by "material," we insist on some solid reality of the sort that is definitively resistant to the touch. The microcosmic order does not offer nuclear physicists the kind of distinction we meet in everyday life where a marble table meets the shin so much more sharply than, say, the smell of roses meets the nose. In the microcosmic order as nuclear physicists now understand it, probabilities are the best we'll ever get, *not* because our measuring rods are too crude but rather because the entities to be discovered are more like aromas than marble tables. Indeterminate by nature and not just as a function of our subjective ignorance, they look more like smears than dots, more like trends than singular events, more like tendencies than hard facts.

When aggregated, these microcosmic probabilistic events add up to virtual certainties in everyday life. Drop a television on your toe and it *will* hurt. Nor is Heisenberg's uncertainty principle a sufficient argument for free will. I do not want to fall into the trap of defending human freedom on the basis of a critique of physical determinism. In invoking chaos theory I don't want to prove too much. I *don't* want to argue that, because physical matter is not as we thought it was, *therefore* life is uncertain and goals imponderable. To argue in this way is to fall into precisely the kind of bottom-up causality that the case for sublimation sets out to defeat. Physics doesn't dictate ideology. Matter doesn't determine psychology. So arguments from the laboratory cannot be invoked to justify a new ideology or a new psychology. Schrödinger's wave equation is *still* insufficient for finding love.

We get it wrong when we zoom in to particular cases from the abandonment of absolutes at the outer horizons of everyday life—just as I got it wrong when I expected Schrödinger's wave equation to help me on dates at Bennington. But, in addition to the question of *scale,* there is also the question of *approach:* do we come at these questions of ethics from the point of view of the (albeit now chastened and more modest) engineer with a calculator?

Here we must call upon the skills of artists and poets, among whom we find the skill for dealing with *ambiguity and duplicity.* Newton's inverse square law is always and everywhere the same. Two bodies *must* attract each other inversely as the square of their distance, always and everywhere in the universe. But male and female human beings do not attract each other with anywhere near the same uniform necessity. Contingency creeps into their relationships through the door marked "custom, culture, and the sublimations of civilization."

The scandal of Goallessness demands that we wrestle with the question of good and evil, *but that we do so in the context of the sublime.* The outcome is far from definitive. In the absence of the

Grand Goals provided by religion and ideology, the individual is thrown back on humbler resources like the literary critic's skill at interpreting texts where no definitive reading, no final conclusion, no perfect solution is ever reached. Each unwanted pregnancy has its own unique consequences; each Supreme Court case calls for judgments backed by wisdom, not just calculations of uncertain consequences. *Interpretation in the symbolic order is different from calculation in the physical order.* Measurements and calculations of quantities tend to converge incrementally toward ever more accurate results as our tools become ever more precise. But interpretations can flip back and forth from one extreme to another. "Did she *really* mean it? Or was she being sarcastic?"

This difference between interpretation and calculation has import for the way we set and reach our goals. Is Spike inching ever closer to love each time he kisses sweet Cindy, as if each kiss were incrementally adding to the volume of his heart? Or will he wake up one day after she's gone only to realize—shazzam—that it wasn't just habit? He loved her after all! How was he to know? He hardly knew the meaning of the word, such are the confusions of its use in our pop culture.

Customs are the work of cultures, and culture is the product of sublimation. And sublimation is the work of minds that use symbols, memories and associations to weave a complex fabric of meaning. How a flower, a piece of lace, a patch of song or a particular word can make the heart beat faster—these are mysteries that only the several meanings of sublimation can unlock. By applying a few tools from information theory and semiotics, I hope to clarify the significance of sublime symbols for living without a Goal. Raising the fugue on sublimation to the semiotic register, we'll hear how a note played in one harmonic context can sound dissonant in another. The same note —or word—can flip discontinuously from one harmonic (or moral) meaning to another. Claims of love can be cruel jokes. An element of arbitrariness, ambiguity and downright trickery will creep in through the door marked "custom, culture, and the sublimations of civilization." For behind that door sits . . . the Semiotic Gambler.

We need to meet the Semiotic Gambler to learn the secrets of good and evil in a world of signs and symbols. The Semiotic Gambler can tell us how a shift in context can change the meaning of a note or a word or a sign much more radically than a shift in the font measurement of the sign itself. He will help us to appreciate the oscillations of scandal and temptation. He will allow us to make the transition from simple-minded utility in the physical order to the subtleties of the sublime. Physics is morally innocent. There is no evil in physics. Physical facts simply are what they are. There is nothing good or bad about them. Only the actions of symbol users enter the moral realm. And those actions are always subject to the threat of evil, because part of what turns a physical movement—say the wave of a hand—into an *action* (like a salutation) is a conscious intention; and the intention of an action, to the extent that it can be articulated in words, is always open to interpretation and the possibility of *doubling*.

THE SEMIOTIC GAMBLER

Semiotics is the study of signs. All signs. Road signs, billboards, numbers, letters, words, gestures, status symbols, you name it. Whatever signifies (*sign*-ifies) something other than itself is a possible subject for the discipline called semiotics. Just as flowers can have symbolic significance, so can cars or clothes or furniture that functions as a "fashion statement." Linguistics alone will tell us about the meaning of words, but a more inclusive semiotics can help us interpret fashion statements, manners and the mixed messages we get from our sometime friends who might be engaging in genuine praise . . . or is it manipulative flattery? Scholars will nitpick over the difference between semiotics and semiology, but for our purposes we needn't bother. The point I want to make is so crude that I call attention to it with the unscientific, rhetorical device of personification: I invoke the Semiotic Gambler.

Who, pray, is this Semiotic Gambler? Imagine him as like God in the story of the Tower of Babel, except that the Semiotic Gambler didn't give all the different tribes different languages as a punishment for their hubris in trying to build their way to heaven. He just scattered syllables where they may so that, come the twentieth century, English lovers say "I love you," German lovers say *"Ich liebe dich,"* French lovers say *"Je t'aime,"* and so on. They all *mean* roughly the same thing—which is by no means easy to pin down very precisely. But they use different sounds and syllables to say it. The Semiotic Gambler is the god who, contrary to Einstein's claim, *does* play dice.

The point to be made by personifying the figure of the Semiotic Gambler was made by the grandfather of modern semiotics, Ferdinand de Saussure. He labeled it, *"the arbitrariness of the sign."* It's a point of such simplicity that professors of linguistics often introduce it on the first day of class and then take it for granted without pausing to note that *it changes everything.* Its ripple effects extend throughout the entire curriculum and beyond, to those dark moments of passion where lovers dare or dare not invoke words of love. This one stroke of De

Saussure's intellect divides the physical sciences from the humanities forever. But more important, it distinguishes the invention of our humanity from the mastery of nature. De Saussure's move shines light into the chasm that separates nature from culture, the natural from the artificial, the physics of the physical realm from the semiotics of the symbolic realm, and the scientific measurement of quantity from the semiotic interpretation of moral quality.

Why is the arbitrariness of the sign so earth-shakingly significant to our understanding of living without a Goal? If the goals we set derive much of their meaning from symbols—as is surely the case with goals like love or fame—then the source of meaning for our symbols is the source of meaning for our goals. We need to know how symbols gain their meaning. If language were tightly tied to a solid world, then symbols could be trusted to have the solidity of the world they represent. Not only is the world not as solid as some materialists once thought it to be, but language is tied more loosely to it than linguists used to believe.

ONCE UPON A time linguists thought they could tie language very tightly to the world with three nonarbitrary devices: (1) sound-alikes or *onomatopoeia;* (2) pointing and naming, or *ostension;* and (3) the evolution of language, or *etymology.* Then along came Ferdinand de Saussure.

Prior to Ferdinand de Saussure, linguistics had been mired for centuries in the misguided attempt to find the laws of *necessary* connection between the sounds of words and the things they represent. They wanted to find a firm foundation for linguistic meaning by basing it on some reference to an Absolute, whether in objective reality, or in some ethereal realm of Platonic meanings. This effort goes all the way back to the Platonic dialogue, the *Cratylus,* in which Socrates and his friends explore the relationships between the sounds of words and the things they represent, and to pictographic languages like Egyptian hieroglyphics in which a little picture of a fish *means,* sure enough, "fish."

As for spoken language rather than written language, the attempt may seem a little more difficult. After all, we have an awkward but very impressive-sounding word to name a whole class of fairly obvious sound-alikes in language: we call them *onomatopoeic.* Or, to be much cruder and clearer about it, just call it *the bow-wow theory of language.* We know that "bow-wow" refers to the sounds dogs make because it *sounds like* the sounds dogs make. "Bow-wow" is *not* arbitrarily related to the barking of dogs. There is a physical similarity of sound that is as obvious as the physical similarity of shape that binds the hieroglyphic picture of a fish to real fish.

Semiotics pursued two other linkages to tie words nonarbitrarily to things: etymology and the act of pointing. Like the obviousness of the link between "bow-wow" and a dog's bark, the act of pointing, while saying, "Me Tarzan, you Jane," was thought sufficient to ground the meaning of some first words. These *ostensive* definitions were supposed to confer meaning by the baptismal act of pointing and naming. A primitive vocabulary could be generated by the nonarbitrary, physical relationships of pointing or imitating by sound. Then the meanings of later words could be explained by the equally nonarbitrary linkages uncovered by *etymology.*

In the parlor game called telephone, a word or phrase is

whispered around a circle from one ear to the next, changing, sometimes hilariously, as it travels. "Little Jack Horner" becomes "hit the rack in the corner," or whatever. Linguists searching for the meanings of modern languages by finding nonarbitrary connections between older words and things came to look upon language as a centuries-old game of telephone. This approach seemed to explain why so few words today can be understood by either the bow-wow theory or ostension. They could preserve the illusion of a nonarbitrary, physical connection between words and things by invoking various combinations of onomatopoeia, ostension and etymology.

Then along came De Saussure, who saw through the charade of looking at language as a long game of telephone. He broke with the attempt to preserve nonarbitrary linkages and invited us to look at each language as all of a piece today. Then we will see that *"rot"* (in German) means "red" (in English), *not* because they sound alike, *not* because the lineage of either or both can be traced to some primitive act of naming, but because *"rot" plays the same role* in Germany today as "red" plays in English-speaking countries, namely, as the name of the color of most ripe apples, fire engines and British telephone booths. *"Rot"* is *used* the same way "red" is used. As Wittgenstein showed, the meaning of a term is to be found in its *use*, not in some one-to-one linkage with a timeless Platonic idea of its meaning. And how the *use* of the word "love" has been diluted!

The meaning of "red" has nothing to do with the sound of the word when spoken or the shape of the word when written. We might as well say *"slint"* for "red" and *"pok"* for "blue." If, by some instantaneous word-processing search-and-change, we could hit a key and replace every single instance of "red" with "slint" and "blue" with "pok," then there would be no confusion whatever. For everyone would *know* that "slint" denoted the color of ripe apples, and "pok" the color of a cloudless sky, and the two, together with "white," the colors of the American flag, and there would be no confusion.

This little thought experiment runs into some trouble when we take it as far as revising the history of English and American poetry: "Roses are slint, violets are pok . . ." and then what? But that only goes to show the difference between the *poetic* use of language, in which the physical sounds of words *do* make a difference to their appropriate usage, and ordinary nonpoetic language in which the physical shape of the sign has an *arbitrary* relationship to its meaning.

De Saussure went on to explain how language works in terms of language's structure at a simultaneous slice across time. Words have meaning not by virtue of one-to-one, nonarbitrary relationships to things, nor by virtue of inheriting meanings through time; instead, words hold their meanings by virtue of *the place they hold* in the vast latticework of today's language. Each word marks *a place* in the language, a stable address in the lace. And it is the language as a whole, the entire veil, that gives each word its meaning, not the shape or sound of any word all by itself.

Words, as signs, are not like self-subsistent things that can persist through a change of location. Words are more like numbers than rocks. You can take a rock from New York to Chicago and it is still the same rock. If you move the number 9 from its location between 8 and 10 to a new location between 3 and 5, then it is legitimate to claim that it's not 9 at all anymore, but 4. If a child insists on counting 1,2,3,9,5 . . . you will patiently point out, "No, 4 comes between 3 and 5; 9 comes after 8 and before 10." The address is located by its neighbors, not by its name. So, likewise, with words: the neighborhood, the context, makes all the difference. When it comes to accounting for the meanings of words, remember the three laws of value in real estate: location, location and location.

De Saussure saw all of this very clearly, and to those who understood the significance of his insight, the study of ancient languages ceased being a cousin to archaeology. No longer was the *shape* of a word, like the shape of an unearthed piece of crockery, the clue to its meaning. Nor was etymology as important as it had been. Instead linguists began uncovering the structures evident in *today's* use of language: they started mapping linguistic neighborhoods without worrying all that much about how they came to be the way they are, or about what building materials (which letters) were used to build each home (each word). Semiotics stopped worrying about the linear melody of etymology and started listening for the harmonies that could be heard among many words at any given moment in time. This shift of analytic approach—*from* the quest for historical origins through etymology *to* the recognition of simultaneous patterns across a slice of time—might look like a minor theoretical wrinkle in a relatively arcane discipline. But its implications for the understanding of human consciousness are immense: with this single stroke we are set loose from what might have been the firm foundations of historical origins. We are robbed of original essence and released to find meaning in contemporary existence. Morality is cut loose from theories of *human nature* because the meanings of our actions are defined by *human culture*. And cultures change and differ from one another.

The fiction of the Semiotic Gambler needn't be taken too literally. Einstein wasn't talking theology when he said that God didn't play dice. He was using the language of parable to make a claim about physics—that the physical world is perfectly deterministic: that it is governed by laws that describe nonarbitrary, binding relationships among physical things. What goes up *must* come down—every time. So, likewise, take the fiction of the Semiotic Gambler as a way of describing the fact that the relationship between physical things and language is, with a few misleading exceptions (like onomatopoeia and a few subtleties of phonology), largely *arbitrary*.

SEMIOTICS AND SUBLIMATION

Once one has appreciated the whimsy of the Semiotic Gambler and fully absorbed the significance of the arbitrariness of the sign, then the relationship between physical sexuality and its sublimation in the language of love is completely different. The sublimation of sexuality has nothing to do with leaving the body behind on a Platonic flight toward the Goal of the sublime. Nor is there a need for Freud's cold shower. The point is not at all to transcend the physical. The point is rather to heighten the sheer trembling excitement of physical desire by hearing its echoes in different registers of meaning and significance: sex the way Ned likes it, with eyes open and a mind working, aware of inhibitions and the temptation to transgression. The stronger the original physical impulse, the more likely sublime resonances will be induced. It's a good thing Spike's hormones work. Now all he needs to do is find the higher registers.

The doubling achieved in symbolism is more like the duplicity of a *double entendre* than the physical repetition of an echo. It is in a grammatical space like language that the erotic resonates. The mind starts driving the hormones, not just the hormones driving the mind. The cultivation of sexuality from animal reproduction to the heights of eroticism follows a strict grammar. Certain things go together in certain naughty and exciting ways, like stockings and garter belts. Like the grammar of language, this erotic grammar allows an infinite number of new sentences to be formed. Also like language, this erotic grammar has one foot in the physical and one foot in the sublime.

De Saussure's discovery *changes everything,* from sexuality to economics. By supplying the crucial link in an argument for a new understanding of sublimation, De Saussure has given us the clue to a new appreciation of the sublime. No longer is the sublime to be worshiped as an actual realm that transcends human experience like the nonbodily blueprint-in-the-sky of Platonism. Now the sublime is *possible,* but only if we creatively achieve it. No longer is the sublime to be derided as a pale shadow of a reality that is all and only material. Now the sublime is as real as matter, but it takes a mind to recognize and interpret it. No longer is the language of love a pale shadow or distorted representation of *the real thing.* Now the language of love enhances and heightens the physical sensations on which it's based. No longer is the cultivation of instinct into art just a redirection of vital energies into effete reflections. Now these "reflections" actually illuminate and magnify the instincts that were their origin. No longer is the sublimation of eros its emasculation, as if hot tropical juices were being allowed to cool as they dissipate into tepid pools and run off through northern channels. Now the sublimation of eros can be sexier than the rising sap of adolescent desire.

Nor does it make sense to link different colors of lace with different messages by a series of nonarbitrary, literalistic, Pavlovian associations in a stimulus-response theory of seduction, an onomatopoetics of lace, a woof-woof theory of lingerie. Each of these physicalistic images of the relationship between biology and the sublime utterly misses the earth-shaking discontinuity that divides the physical from the semiotic—the vast gulf opened up by De Saussure's discovery of the arbitrariness of the sign.

By opening up this gap, De Saussure led the field of linguistics away from a preoccupation with singular origins—Adam and Eve words—and toward a concern with structural relationships in today's language. But these structures still relate one word to another. He didn't take a leap into Plato's ethereal realm of pure ideas. Instead the sublime has an existence that is altogether its own, a tracery of relationships that is no more derivative from and inferior to physical existence than lace is inferior to Gore-Tex. Again, lace is *not supposed* to keep out the rain.

The good news about this reinterpretation of sublimation based on semiotics is that we *can* get more out of less. Just as the quick-witted get more out of life by seeing the humorous side where the literal-minded miss the joke, so the erotically erudite will be incited to passion by what leaves others cold. By being aware of the multiple meanings of each moment and the different scales and registers of significance, the lively mind lives in a richer world. Blinkered by "the single vision of Newton's sleep," focused on the narrow destination of a single Goal, utilitarian functionaries keep plodding straight ahead like robots that have been programmed toward a single destination.

SEMIOTICS AND THE ORIGIN OF EVIL

Now for the bad news that follows from De Saussure's liberation of symbols from nonarbitrary tethers to things. Evil is inevitable because its source is to be found among the most innocent. The origin of evil is to be found in the play of innocents, in the joke gone wrong. *The origin of evil is to be found in play and teasing and joking around.* Sometimes the naughty slides down toward decadence. The playful teasing that *could* be an act of love becomes instead a step toward depravity.

A joke, in order to *be* a joke, always requires duplicity, some sort of *double entendre,* some play on words or switch of context that places an entirely different significance on the punch line. In every piece of humor there is always some sort of *doubling.* To the extent that play involves or is like humor, like *playing a joke on someone,* then it is intrinsically the case that the joke *can* be misunderstood. Unless it is genuinely and successfully ambiguous to begin with, it cannot be a good joke. But the line between a good joke and a bad joke is often very fine.

This structure of humor and play predetermines the inevitability of the play going wrong sooner or later. And as soon as the joke goes wrong, as soon as someone doesn't get the joke, doesn't *take it in fun,* then an injury has been committed, to which there may be a response in kind, then a further reaction, then reprisals, then revenge, then recriminations, then yet crueler revenge . . . and by then anything can happen, even evil. And it all started because of a joke. "I really didn't mean to hurt you," one protests. "It was only a joke. . . ." But the seeds of evil have already been sown.

Finding the origin of evil in the play of innocents is bad

news because it means we can never eradicate evil once and for all. The seeds of evil lie ready to sprout in every discourse, in every set of symbolic relationships that allows itself to reach outside the narrowly literal.

Literalism seemed appropriate in an industrial-material order of *things* rather than *signs.* Not all that glitters is really gold, and it pays to have ways to determine the difference between 14-karat and 18-karat purity. In the symbolic order things are not always so definitive. But as soon as literalism allows an inch to allegory, metaphor, irony or any of the other rhetorical tropes, evil can arise when someone fails to appreciate the playfulness of a literary device. If you don't get the joke, if the second level of a double meaning never occurs to you and you go ahead blindly accepting the first as the entirety of my intention, then you fail to understand my true intentions. And the consequence of your failure to understand my true intention means that you will attribute to me some intention that changes the meaning of my acts in your eyes.

This entire dynamic can be laid at the doorstep of the Semiotic Gambler. It's *his* doing, his fault. The moment you enter the semiotic realm, the moment material things become signs and sprout another level of *meanings* that have nothing to do with their physical shapes as *things,* then you've given the Semiotic Gambler an opportunity to fiddle around with those meanings in ways that have little to do with the innocent ways of physical necessity.

What can we do to keep play from turning evil? Turn play into games with rules. Don't just challenge their gang to see whether your gang can get the coconut between the palm trees, no holds barred. Create some rules—like the rules of soccer or football—so that you don't kill each other in the course of having fun. That way we sublimate play into a more structured environment. In a game, the range of possible intentions is sufficiently circumscribed so that, even where duplicity remains crucial—the athlete's feint in one direction before going in another—the range of possible interpretations does not include the defamation, torture, heartbreak or murder of the other competitor.

Once we begin to circumscribe play with rules, we are on the way toward culture with all of its customs, rules and regulations. Politics is the practice of negotiating the rules of the games we play. The paradox of postmodernism consists in the fact that *politics, which are increasingly symbol-laden and mediated, are both necessary and perverse.* We must have political institutions to circumscribe the rules of play; but the political institutions themselves have a way of creating and compounding evil through the lumbering momentum of well-intended initiatives that produce unintended side effects in addition to, or in place of, their intended goals. Especially as we move out of the industrial-political era and enter the information-economic era, we find ourselves confronted again and again by the politics of irony, which is where this chapter began. But now it should be clear that politics produces ironies not only because the state is so *large,* but also because the state is too much of a *machine.*

The state is not sublime. The state does not play. The state lacks a sense of humor. Once upon a time politics was an activity shared by human beings in discourse with one another. In Periclean Athens, political discourse was a shared act of deliberation, an almost artistic endeavor of a community to make it up as it went along. Now both the genius of Athens and the genius of *the Constitution* are as solidified in memory as *Beethoven's Fifth* is fixed as "a classic." And there is some danger that, confusing culture with nature, we will become imprisoned by a belief in the rigidity of what we respect.

Freedom demands that we have a vivid sense of the plasticity of the human condition. The laws of physics may not bend to the human will, but the rules we fashion for the games we play are subject to human modification. Transgression tests the rules and reminds us of both their power *and* their plasticity. Ned risks the embarrassment of Lila calling him a fetishist. Artists are testing the boundaries of propriety all the time. There is no science of transgression. Very little is guaranteed, not the morning paper delivery, not the milkman, not the mailman, not even love.

The experience of Goallessness requires a very particular kind of philosophy: not a philosophy of scientific proofs and guarantees, but an aesthetics that addresses the question of how to live *without* proofs and guarantees. Precisely to the extent that Goals are not objectively *given* like the difference between sheep and goats, precisely to the extent that Goals are not simply *there* to be picked up and lived like a well-defined job description, precisely to that extent one's goals must be set according to an ongoing accretion of experience, judgment and creativity. Living without a Goal calls for an artful life.

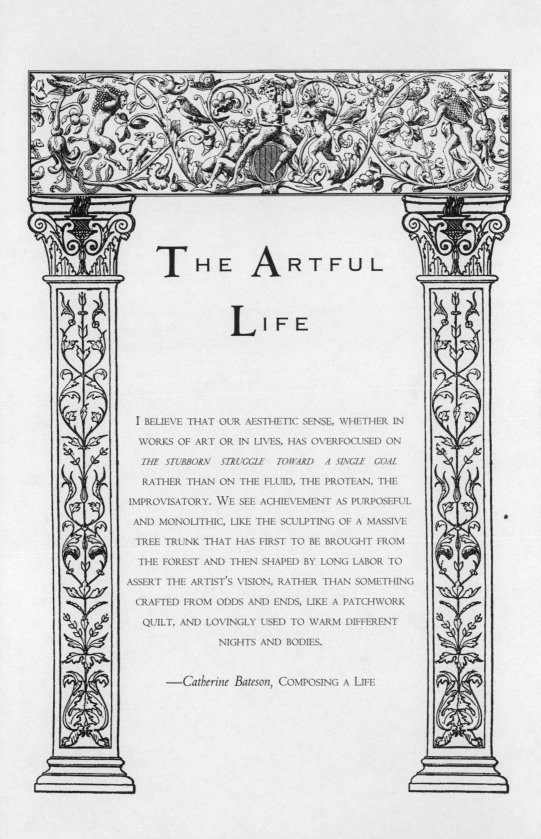

THE ARTFUL LIFE

I BELIEVE THAT OUR AESTHETIC SENSE, WHETHER IN
WORKS OF ART OR IN LIVES, HAS OVERFOCUSED ON
THE STUBBORN STRUGGLE TOWARD A SINGLE GOAL
RATHER THAN ON THE FLUID, THE PROTEAN, THE
IMPROVISATORY. WE SEE ACHIEVEMENT AS PURPOSEFUL
AND MONOLITHIC, LIKE THE SCULPTING OF A MASSIVE
TREE TRUNK THAT HAS FIRST TO BE BROUGHT FROM
THE FOREST AND THEN SHAPED BY LONG LABOR TO
ASSERT THE ARTIST'S VISION, RATHER THAN SOMETHING
CRAFTED FROM ODDS AND ENDS, LIKE A PATCHWORK
QUILT, AND LOVINGLY USED TO WARM DIFFERENT
NIGHTS AND BODIES.

—*Catherine Bateson*, COMPOSING A LIFE

9

HE PROCESS OF COMPOSING A
life is very much like the process of creat-
ing a work of art. While it is arguably
pretentious to think of yourself as "a
work of art"—the phrase carries connotations of ceremonial
display, the framing and museuming of the precious self—it
remains true that much about creating art applies equally well
to cultivating a self: the demand for uniqueness combined with
the requirement of using stock pieces for at least part of the
construction; the vertiginous freedom of expression once one
has been released from the demand for photographic literalism;
the anxiety of influence induced by those who have gone before,
shown the way, but cannot be followed footprint for footprint
for fear of falling into mere copying.

Living artfully should not be confused with pursuing the Goal of absolute beauty. Nor would I encourage the pretentiousness of the aesthete who claims that his life *is* art. The aesthete—oddly, ironically—is guilty of literalism, of trying to model life too closely on art. Better to take artistic creation as a *metaphor:* to see in the challenge of artistic creativity a model or a *likeness* for the challenge of living life without a Goal.

The task of the artist is *like* the task of living, both in having no goal or end outside itself and in having no guarantee of success. Further, life and art both call for a balance of freedom and discipline. Both life and art take place in real time. Both build on what has gone before. Both demand an ability to bend the momentum of tradition toward the unprecedented. Both require creativity.

HOW IS ONE to choose among the lesser goals that comprise life's patchwork quilt? If life without a single Goal is something like quilting, then how big are the pieces likely to be? How near and how far are the goals that survive the obsolescence of absolutes? If the impressive tapestries of ultimate Goals are no longer available, we run the risk of being thrown back on the thread's-width immediacy of the moment. Then all of our motivations would derive from the push of immediate impulse rather than the pull of some religious or ideological destiny. Does Nietzsche's "goallessness as such" leave us unable to make any plans whatever?

This business of Goallessness is vulnerable to ridicule. "Goallessness": the word calls up an image of people sitting around an office with nothing to do; management by nonobjectives; a serious threat of boredom; a terminal listlessness that settles over society like a sultry tropical night. Of course we will have goals, many of them, which we will patch together like the quilt in the quote from Catherine Bateson. And we will pursue those various goals in the various rhythms they require, some very short-term, some longer-term. After all, the idea of living day to day, hour to hour, with no goals at all is ludicrous. If you make Goallessness a *rule* rather than the principle of a faith, then you will not get much done.

We must be able to cast some of our actions at least as far as the time it takes for sweet william to bloom from seed—two growing seasons at least. Otherwise we would never achieve any of the fruits of cultivation or culture that require coordination, planning, discipline, practice. We would never hear a symphony. Goallessness cannot be a *rule*, just the principle of a faith.

The clever reader may be thinking: *Ah, this is where he's going to take it all back. He started with a bold thesis: Goallessness. Now, in the face of all of the obvious counterexamples, he's going to weaken the thesis to something innocuous enough for anyone to accept.* No, I'm not going to take it all back. In order to show how Goallessness can be the principle of our faith, even as we pursue and achieve many patchwork goals, this chapter turns to the creation of art as a metaphor for living without a Goal.

ART AND ETHICS

I have fixed on art as a guide if not a rule. Art has no end outside itself. A work of art does no work. It is not *for the sake of* anything else. Having nothing to gain on any specific behalf, art does not serve purposes beyond itself. If it tries to preach on behalf of some particular interest, it falls into propaganda. Rather than fine art, it becomes decoration for doctrine. As overearnest students of art are told, "Got a message? Send a telegram." So, likewise, one avoids the kind of life that would reduce each gesture to a step closer to some single, obvious Goal.

The dramas and difficulties of artistic creation are very much like the difficulties confronted in the creation of the self. This is why aesthetics and ethics are more similar to one another than either is to science or mathematics. Aesthetics and ethics are about the judgment of the unique and particular, while science and mathematics are about the laws of the universal and repeatable, which human life never is.

In making this case for the closeness of the good and the beautiful I am perhaps stating the obvious. Yet the journals of academic philosophy and the casuistry of professional ethicists (what a horrible word!) suggest an almost universal adherence to a code of consequential rationality in thrall to simple-minded linear logic. I do not deny that the heart has its reasons or the passions their strategies. But the swirls of my emotions are more like the whorls of clouds over the Pacific than the circuit diagrams for my computer. The low-pressure depression to the left of my emotional map will probably mean tears tomorrow, but who knows? The probabilities are more impressionistic than calculable.

Our ethical and aesthetic judgments are not separable from their influences as conclusions are separable from premises. It is not a matter of Step One and Step Two guaranteeing that we proceed to Step Three. Picasso's *Guernica* is not beautiful *because* it contains some particular motifs; its beauty consists in the commingling of all its motifs. Neither is my behavior good or bad *because* it produced benign effects or derived from particular intentions. Our judgments spring from perceptions that are less syllogistic than the calculations of logicians. This is not to say that they are irrational, or that they admit of no defense whatever. But the defenses we give for our moral decisions will look less like logical proofs and more like literary criticism.

The work of the contemporary artist—neither under contract to the Church nor beholden to the literal representation of reality—mimics a life that has no clear measure of success. True, the postmodern artist can make literalistic gestures by using photography or pop images from the worlds of advertising and entertainment. But these representational gestures are tinged with irony in a way that nineteenth-century portraits and landscapes were not.

So, likewise, the artful life can draw on the accounts laid up by science and religion. One useful measure is physical health; another might be some sense of humility before something that is bigger than you are. But the artful incorporation of different elements in a postmodern life will be every bit as devoid of secure foundations in reality as a work of contemporary art is removed from the simple representation of a landscape. The old measuring rods for life—How big is your family? How many head of cattle do you own?—are as obsolete as literal representation in art. *For, just as art has surrendered to photography the job of literal representation, so life has surrendered to technology the job of fulfilling simply definable functions with clearly describable goals.*

I HEAR BEETHOVEN'S Fifth as *Beethoven's Fifth.* How did Beethoven first hear it? How do I hear my life? Sometimes I succeed in making it up as I go along. Sometimes I listen for directions from elsewhere; not from politicians, even less from priests. I have allowed myself a few mid-course corrections: a switch of career from teaching to consulting. I have been through a divorce. I cannot justify these moves according to some larger scheme. They seemed like good ideas at the time. Could an artist say more about just *why* she placed *that* color just *there?*

The artist lives with blank pages and blank canvases, not even sure whether canvas will be the medium of the next creation. It might be an arrangement of ropes, or the reordering of some previously printed material, or the excavation of some land, or a simple act of writing. The rest of us expect the canvas to be full before it has a role in our lives. If you approach each day as an artist approaches a blank canvas, neither painting by the numbers according to someone else's design, nor trying to represent some scene with the faithfulness of photography, then you confront the challenge of creativity. Why dip into the yellow rather than the blue? Is there any real reason to be a butcher or a baker? The *reasons,* such as they are, turn out to have more to do with the integrity of the whole—the whole artwork or the whole life—than with any Goal or interest that lies outside either artwork or life. Neither beauty nor happiness can be guaranteed by following some set of precise rules for the arrangement of means to an end.

Creativity relies less on goal-directed labor than on a subtle mix of discipline and play. The artist suffers under an imperative to delight, an obligation to bask in pleasure. Someone must scout those frontiers of bliss and discover the pitfalls. There are risks. It is not an accident that artists suffer accidents. It is in the nature of the case that they take risks. But if one must take risks, what better place than in pleasure's paradise?

Hanging over my desk is a plaque by the artist Jenny Holzer, the creator of the widely displayed aphorism, "Protect me from what I want." The one on my wall reads, "Finding extreme pleasure will make you a better person if you're careful about what thrills you." But how does one take risks carefully?

I have risked the bliss of sublime Goallessness, but I find the feeling difficult to communicate. There is a reason why there is so little good writing about ecstasy: the gods and goddesses don't like lovers who kiss and tell. But someone has to report back from the outer frontiers of human delight. Someone must be willing to say: *These are the Blessed Isles. Put down your anchor here and know bliss.* Somebody must report back from paradise. Otherwise how will the rest of us know when we have found it?

Those of us who are Protestant, or Jewish, or Japanese usually have a built-in governor on our capacity for delight. Our level of pleasure cannot rise above a certain point without an automatic inhibitor kicking in. Intellectuals of whatever faith find it unfashionable to admit happiness. Nietzsche snarled about "wretched contentment." But he also sang about the "Blessed Isles."

Not just our ambivalences toward bliss and pleasure but also the familiar themes of art and humor offer examples of the way goal-directed behavior can defeat itself. Each serves notice on the dangers of offering cookbook recipes for how to live without a Goal. A ten-step method for living without a Goal will fail just as surely as a joke laboriously explained.

The themes I've been weaving together here in this coda to the fugue—art, humor and the pursuit of pleasure—have the disturbing aura of an apology for luxury and extravagance at a time when the earth can ill afford it. But in the realm of the sublime, extravagance is not only allowed but required. We need to shift more of our commerce from the metabolism of need, mass, work and production to the metabolism of desire, the sublime, play and consumption. But we will not do so until we give up some of our old goals of accumulation and mastery over matter.

THE SCANDAL OF DELIGHT

In an information economy, the logic of production and accumulation in the industrial and agricultural eras gives way— even if only gradually—to an experiential logic of consumption. This revolutionary insight is so perverse from the point of view of traditional virtue that it could only come from the French. And so it is that Georges Bataille, in *The Accursed Share*, observes: "Henceforth what matters *primarily* is no longer to develop the productive forces but to spend their products sumptuously. . . . I insist on the fact that there is generally no growth but only a luxurious squandering of energy in every form! The history of life on earth is mainly the effect of a wild exuberance; the dominant event is the development of luxury." And elsewhere: "Whether the writer wants it or not, the spirit of literature always sides with squandering, *with the absence of definite goals.*"

Bataille is saying that the spirit of literature lives on exuberant freedom, not the careful calculation of means and resources necessary to reach a predetermined goal. If humanity is most human in its freedom rather than in its satisfaction of bare necessities, then it is precisely the *unnecessary*—the luxurious— that is necessary to humanity. The so-called "basic necessities" are necessary to keep the animal in us alive. But luxuries are necessary to keep alive what is free and creative. With the transition from a physical to a semiotic economy, what was formerly scandalous—a sacrificial exuberance and squandering of resources—now becomes essential.

While this idea may appear mad to minds still bound by the logic of material acquisition and capital accumulation, it enjoys a certain sanity in the context of an economics of information and experience. Jean Baudrillard, writing decades later than Bataille, turned Marxism on its head by showing how its categories are inadequate to a symbolic economy because they were derived from the industrial era of material production. More clearly than Bataille, Baudrillard assimilated the significance of the semiotic turn, so it was easier for him to articulate the turn from production to consumption: "The first stage of the analysis was to conceptualize consumption as an extension of the sphere of productive forces. But now we must do the reverse. We need to conceptualize the whole sphere of production, labour, and productive forces as tilted towards the sphere of 'consumption.'"

Because information does not inform unless it is received, it does not exist until it is consumed. It exists only in its assimilation and dies when it becomes redundant. *Information is intrinsically sacrificial.* What seemed mad and illogical in the old order of production becomes sane and logical in the new order of semiotic consumption. So, for example, the "insanity" of sacrifice, of giving something for nothing, becomes the royal road to the sublime, not an altruistic act of self-denial. While some musicians try to forbid taping at their concerts, or the circulation of bootleg cassettes, others like the Grateful Dead and Peter Gabriel encourage what becomes free advertising.

THE CHANGING NATURE OF
''OWNERSHIP''

With the transition from an industrial to an information economy, the nature of ownership and possession—and hence accumulation—changes. Ownership and accumulation no longer
have much to do with the physical possession of things and the
mastery of matter. The notion of ownership that was modeled
on the appropriation and possessive keeping of more and more
of the same physical stuff now gives way to the primacy of a
capacity for discernment and appreciation. The metabolism of
sublime desire has more to do with a quickening of consciousness, an awakening of taste, a capacity for making differentiations that articulate truly human experience into the refinement
of delight.

Ownership now has more to do with the heat of real-time
experience than with the cold storage of stuff. As the very
nature of property shifts from physical goods and real estate
toward experiences and more ephemeral goods like words and
images, books and movies, art, travel . . . the idea of "ownership" begins to unravel at the edges. When I enjoy a movie or
appreciate a play or, in the extreme case, take delight in a
sunset, is the question of ownership even relevant to the wealth
I experience?

Ephemeral experiences cannot be accumulated in the same
way that wheat can be stored in a silo. They cannot be owned
the way one used to own forty acres, or four hundred head of
cattle, or a dozen camels, or a pot of gold. Ownership can no
longer be counted out quite so easily when, for example, it is a
question of clean air. Ownership is difficult in cases of snatches
of a song, or a plot, or a piece of software. With ephemeral

goods and services, ownership claims are harder to settle than in cases of stolen cars.

This changing nature of ownership is relevant to the practice of Goallessness. For it was the nature of ownership and accumulation in the materialistic old days of the agricultural and industrial eras that got us hooked on certain kinds of goal-directed activity in the first place. Recall Aesop's fable of the industrious ants who worked all summer while the irresponsible grasshopper just fiddled the days away. There were those ants, safely regimented, marching in single file, fetching and hauling, working and saving, piling up vast stores for the sake of surviving the long winter. And what was the grasshopper doing? Enjoying the moment. Playing. Singing. Dancing. How reprehensible!

As we make the transition from the agricultural and industrial eras into an information and experience economy, the game does not always go to the goal-directed discipline of ants. Instead, people who explore the outer reaches of human delight, then learn how to bottle and sell some of their ecstasy, end up being far more successful than the drudges who are convinced of their duty to defer gratification forever. Despite his eventual failure to grasp the sublime, Howard Hughes had *fun* making movies. His odd schedule showed that he worked far more by impulse and passion than by duty and routine. He *enjoyed* flying. And he certainly took pleasure in beautiful women. Despite the extent of his wealth on paper, he was sublimely unattached to physical things toward the end of his life—"no sentimental impediments." It's just that, like the Japanese, he had trouble surrendering *control* in the course of having fun.

We picked up this training in goal-directed behavior from

the end of the agricultural era, the era of large silos for storage, the era of the industrialization of agriculture. This training in goal-directed behavior, so logical and rational in days gone by, is no longer appropriate to the nature of ownership and property in the information age. Nor does it describe a pattern of reward we see in our sublimated economy. Low savings rates in the United States suggest that its citizens somehow know that the old storage mentality is obsolete. These days the grasshoppers get rewarded: the kids who sat around playing their guitars all day end up as wealthy rock stars while the poor nerds who did their homework end up as low-paid grunts watching their irresponsible classmates on MTV. The kids who insisted on playing basketball all day may be pulling down millions of dollars playing pro ball. The kids who frittered away their youth as surf bums now own sprawling franchises for beachwear, while the teacher's pet in English class is struggling for tenure at some backwater college in the boondocks.

As long as there remains a fear that there is not enough in the silo, the realm of necessity will continue to tug at our intentions. We will not be free of the goal of freedom from want. So we will line up our tools to increase productivity, and we will do what we can to gain mastery over matter. The fear of want and the goal of freedom from want are so primitive, so deep, that they can drive us to accumulate absurd degrees of wealth and to erect defenses against the claims of others to protect that wealth. The economics of the sublime suggest to me that the old possessiveness may be the greatest enemy of the new wealth.

With the success of the Industrial Revolution, however, the goal of increasing productivity becomes superfluous if not dangerous. To say it once again, we are being overwhelmed by *stuff*, smothered by sheer obesity. The problem, as never before, is not production but consumption. *And neither Narcissus nor his anorexic sisters will eat!*

In living without a Goal, we will encourage consumption *not* because we are ethically callous, ecologically ignorant or morally indifferent about the outcome of our actions, but rather because we are convinced that "the way life works" has less to do with *controlling outcomes* than with a kind of profligate creativity combined with principles of selection by consumption. We will have ceased looking at the world as a mechanistic engineer would—this was Howard Hughes's final limitation—and we will have adopted an *evolutionary, artistic, creative paradigm.*

THE EVOLUTIONARY PARADIGM

The evolutionary model of change and development calls for a new understanding of the role of the random and apparently superfluous. The evolutionary paradigm renders creativity by the route of profligate diversity and a process of selection.

The mechanistic paradigm tries to create according to a plan that leads to a predetermined goal: five steps to guaranteed creativity, not six or seven. Waste not, want not. Husband your resources, and measure productivity as the greatest output for the least input. But creativity does not work this way. Just look at the administration of big science—planned creativity—and then look at its track record for innovation. On a dollar-per-patent basis, big science doesn't do as well as the less bureaucratized passion of garage inventors.

I remember how strange I found the big-science environment at Stanford Research Institute where I worked for seven years. Despite the presence of some remarkably creative people, a lot of the work was managed counterproductively. At budget time each year I would be asked what I planned to do the following year and what it would cost. It always seemed to me that I was being asked what I planned to discover, to which my first answer was, "If I knew, I wouldn't have to discover it." But the bureaucrats were not amused. It was as if the only time genuine discovery would be allowed would be during the month or so of the budget cycle. Because, once the budget was set, there could be no messing around in unbudgeted areas. If you said you were going to research attitudes toward risk, then you'd better not stumble across anything important about attitudes toward time.

The evolutionary paradigm makes the random the friend of rationality, not its enemy. Randomization is the engine of diversity, and diversity turns out to be the mother of invention (not necessity, as the mechanists had thought). Evolution is so creative because it has a constructive role for the random built into its very logic. The process of evolution itself evolved: from mechanical reproduction of more of the same by mitosis, to sexual reproduction by meiosis: from one making two of the very same, to two making one that is different from each. Sex is Mother Nature's little way of making sure that no one gets to play Father God's narcissistic game of reproducing in his own image. Sex is Mother Nature's way of scrambling genes so that every offspring represents a random mixing of different sets of genes rather than the identical reproduction or cloning of same by same.

Variation—profligate variation, and further line extensions on the variations—turns out to be the surest way of coming up with a winner, in Mother Nature's garden as well as in the second nature of the marketplace. New Coke, Classic Coke, Diet Coke, cherry Coke, decaf Coke, decaf Diet Coke . . . and on to the famous coffee klatsch in the movie, *L. A. Story.*

Mechanists produce with a goal. Evolutionists just produce, and produce, like crazy, variation upon variation. Mechanists think they can control the outcomes of their labors. Evolutionists know that differential selection by the environment will determine the relative success of their many offspring, not their creators' goals and intentions. Mechanists try to impose perfect form upon imperfect matter, but the attempt to control matter by the imposition of form—the whole tool-and-die and drill-press metaphysics—has been superseded. Evolution lives without a Goal, and thrives.

WE CANNOT CALCULATE our way to The Good as our Goal any more than I could calculate my way into the good graces of dates at Bennington. That may sound like bad news, but as Dante said of his journey through hell, "I found goodness there." Where? In the warm glow I felt while driving through the dark night after being expelled from Exeter. How's that?

If goodness is not some Goal that awaits us after we jump through all the hoops of some long linear journey, but is instead a perpetually elusive feature of the path itself, then we can no more be expelled from goodness than we can reach it once and for all. The elusiveness of the good follows from its intimacy with evil. We do not find the good by avoiding all evil but by finding our way *through* what *could become* evil if we do not recognize it as such—as, for example, I saw the dangers of German discipline even as I submitted to it. Or as the reluctant narcissist finds his way to love not by retreating into the box canyon of tertiary narcissism but by diving into the extravagant delights of goofing on the self in narcissism degree zero.

We do not find the good by aiming directly at it as a Goal. Like a dim star that disappears when you look right at it, so does goodness disappear when I try to set it clearly apart from evil. Just as Orpheus would lose Eurydice if he looked directly at her, just as Narcissus loses his image in the pond when his lips touch its cool surface, so do I lose the good when I set it as a Goal toward which I aim directly.

The role of the random in evolutionary creativity, and the role of the arbitrary in the way words work and play, both confirm this incalculable elusiveness of The Good. In the realm of the sublime, the near miss may be more beautiful than the direct hit on a destination. In lyrical melodies, dissonances add to a delight that would be lost if the notes only repeated predictable harmonies. Like the height of sexual excitement just prior to orgasm, those sublime dissonances are as essential to the beauty of the whole as the cadences finally reached. Their transgression from what would otherwise be banal harmonies creates lyrical value.

The sublime is tricky, and so much the better. The Semiotic Gambler is a tease who plays dice. I will never achieve a nonarbitrary, literal representation of The Good in language. That's not how words work or play. Instead, the best I can do, and all that I've done, is circle around the elusive center of living without a Goal. "One *cannot grasp the core*" of Henry Miller, wrote Norman Mailer. And so one could say similarly of Goallessness. There is no "geological fundament in the psyche one can call identity" when life is lived in the real time of becoming; and there is no geological fundament to The Good.

To some, this condition of uncertainty feels like nihilism, and in one sense they are right. The old absolutes are gone and science has not replaced them with solid foundations in material reality. But the positive-sum possibilities of sublimation allow for bootstrapping new structures of meaning. The sonata form, the nation-state, works of art and the invention of the corporation all testify to a human capacity for creativity. Songs are possible, but *we* must write them. We cannot hear them behind the wind. In this sense I think of our condition as one of *lyric nihilism.*

Better than a Goal predetermined by God or Nature, I take delight in some of the seemingly random coincidences that shine with sublime significance. I love the fact that Howard Hughes's life was built on the foundation laid by the Hughes *Tool* Company. What a marvelous resonance with the logic of instrumental rationality! I treasure the fact that I came of age behind the wheel of a *Mercury.* It could have been a Ford, but no, that car bore the name of a god who was known as a trickster, a quicksilver messenger who often twisted his messages just a little. I like playing with these archetypal resonances. Of course they *prove* nothing.

AS I COME to these final pages I think of the conversations I've had while writing this book, and of the friends who have reminded me of the obvious paradox: how could completing a book on Goallessness be my goal? If I believed a word of what I was writing, how could I set and attain the goal of completing a book? My answer: it is possible to experience the present as the sustained attainment of a goal rather than as an instrumental means toward that end. Writing this book was a matter of *living with the process of writing,* a perpetual circling that must eventually come to an end.

Much of this book was written in a little flat in London's Mayfair. The location gained a peculiar significance based on experiences long ago. Shortly before my assault on Schrödinger's wave equation I came across the works of Somerset Maugham. I loved *The Razor's Edge* and its portrayal of a young man leaving the comforts of society to seek wisdom, experience and nomadic travels in far-off places and esoteric traditions. Then I read Maugham's autobiography, *The Summing Up.* Though his portrait of his life as a writer appealed to me, it would be inaccurate to claim that I swore an oath to myself, *When I grow up, my goal is to become a writer.* Nonetheless as I went off to my writing studio each morning with a regularity that resembled addiction more than discipline, I could not suppress repeated twinges of delight whenever I passed a plaque commemorating the site where Somerset Maugham lived and wrote some of his best books. That plaque reminded me that I was not engaged in some onerous task toward the realization of some desirable future goal—the completion of this book and whatever rewards it might bring. Instead the very process of completion, the act of writing, the life of a writer, was itself the goal that I had entertained, however tacitly, so many years ago.

What had appealed to me in Maugham's account was not the royalties or the reviews or the overt rewards of the successful writer, but the life, the process, the day-to-day endeavor to render experience sublime through the medium of words. And lo and behold, I spent day after day doing that very thing, albeit with far less grace and much less recognition, just a block from where Maugham himself had plied the trade. So the writing of this book was not so much the pursuit of a goal as it was the practice of a goal already attained: writing—an activity I enjoy.

Yes, there is work. Of course there have been setbacks and frustrations, the anguish at my inability to make the words say what I want them to say, and the opportunities missed, like the sail on San Francisco Bay that my friends are enjoying at this moment. But as I write *these* words, I am aware of the degree to which completing the book was not a goal beckoning from the distance. Writing was a goal whose attainment I've enjoyed with every page, even those many that deservedly landed in the trash.

Goallessness does not preclude accomplishments that others perceive as goals. The *practice* of Goallessness can have tangible outcomes without compromising "the principle of our faith." The present is its own reward . . . and can *still* issue in further rewards that were not the *goal* of the present's practice.

Hollywood has a nice term for those future rewards that may accrue to current contracts: *residuals.* I like to think that, if one devotes oneself to the profligate variation of delights in the present, the residuals will take care of the future. In Hollywood they also say you're only as good as your last movie. They know that the economics of the sublime forbid the accumulation of stable capital.

WHATEVER HAPPENED TO Spike and Lila? Did they meet, fall in love and live happily ever after? Not on your life! Spike and Cindy got married. Though he never loved her all that much in the first place, he gets insanely jealous when others admire her beauty. Lila is less possessive in her love for Ned. Last Valentine's Day she sent him a card that said, without irony, "My love is like the sunset. I glory in his presence. I sit in silence and awe, but I do not say he is *mine.*"

Ownership of the sublime is not like mastery. To own the sublime is not to have and hold forever, till death do you part. Ownership of the sublime is service rather than mastery: less like the love of a possessive husband for his trophy wife, and more like the love of a mother for her children: a nurturing love, stewardship rather than dominion. This nonpossessive love takes delight in the least trace of the beloved, whether the laughter of a child, received as a gift even though not given as such, or the last rays of a sunset streaming magenta over the horizon after the source is long gone.

Even death can be sublime. We would be so much less sad if we learned how to let go of the things we love. Then they might become truly ours for the first time, in this nonpossessive mode that the sublime demands of us. When you go to the movies or read a novel, you invest only the tiniest fraction of what that artwork cost to create. Yet the benefit you derive is immense, despite the fact that you cannot have and hold these artworks as Howard Hughes possessed his millions and kept them from others. This nonpossessive adoration, like the love of parents for their children, combines service, nurturance, stewardship and finally a letting go.

Yes, the earth is ours, our only home. But she is not *mine* in a personally possessive sense. Yes, my dying friend is *my* friend in the most intimate and private sense. And I will miss her when she's gone. But I do not love her better while she is alive by refusing to share her with others. We would be so much less sad if we learned this letting go.

Let go the goal of unnecessary riches at others' expense.

Give up the goal of wealth. You probably have as much money as you need. Much more may bring more trouble, not less.

Let go the goal of total self-sufficiency. You will never achieve it, and you will destroy your relationships with others while trying.

Give up the goal of independence. The world does not work that way. The sublime is relational and interdependent; and anyway, your friends *want* to help you.

Give up the goal of true love. Love, if it is romantic, is never, strictly speaking, true. And if it is not romantic, it is not true love.

Let go the goal of happiness. That sweet bird lights only when least expected.

Let go the goal of fame. Its concave mirror distorts as it amplifies.

Treat these goals and others like them as powerful medicines, useful as prescribed, but dangerous if misused. Keep out of the reach of children.

Acknowledgments

This book owes its birth to two parents and a midwife. It was invited by Harriet Rubin, head of Doubleday Currency. She found me through Napier Collyns, who deserves credit for far more books seeing the light of day than most people will ever know. The midwife—his term, not mine—was Eric Best, a writer whose talent extends beyond his own art to the gift of coaching others. Thanks also to Janet Coleman, who saw the book through its final stages of editing.

Some other friends have suffered earlier drafts, offering the kindness of silence or a few well-chosen words to keep me from embarrassing myself too badly. I want to thank especially Jon McIntire, Michael Murphy, Lawrence Wilkinson, Mary Ellen Klee, and John O'Neil. Others have offered support and encouragement at critical times: Kind words, simple fun, sublime love, or a tender touch. I think of Doris and Karin, Wendy and Ginger, Jessica and Tricia.

There were places crucial to several segments of creation: in addition to Alain Merten's flat in London, Blake's hotel, where these words were written, and the library of the British Museum; Beekman Place in New York; Lake Sunapee, New Hampshire; Esalen Institute on the Big Sur coastline of California; the bar at the Kaimana Beach Hotel in Honolulu; Bon Island off the southern coast of Thailand. Who said literature had to happen only in libraries?

Lastly, thanks to those closest to me, who released me to the acts of solitude that writing requires: Peter Schwartz and Cathleen, and my sons, David and Jonathan.

NOTES

page 1: The lines from Dante are, as stated, from the very opening of *The Inferno.* The translation is my own cobbling together from Tom Phillips's *Dante's Inferno* (London: Thames and Hudson, 1985, p. 10), and the more traditional translation by Charles Eliot Norton, in *Great Books of the Western World* vol. 21 (Chicago: Encyclopaedia Britannica, 1952), I.

page 9: The quote from Tom Wolfe is from his introductory essay to *The Pump House Gang,* reprinted in *Self and World,* ed. James Ogilvy (New York: Harcourt Brace Jovanovich, 1980), 12.

page 10: The quotes from Sartre are from his *Being and Nothingness,* trans. Hazel Barnes (Secaucus, N.J.: Citadel Press, 1977).

page 18: Nietzsche's note on no "being" behind the doing is to be found in *The Genealogy of Morals,* trans. Francis Golffing (Garden City, New York: Doubleday Anchor, 1956), pt. I, sec. xiii, 178f.

page 21: Francis Fukuyama, "The End of History?" in *The National Interest,* Summer, 1989. Since the publication of Fukuyama's famous essay, from which the quotations are taken, Fukuyama has written a very thoughtful book based on his article: *The End of History and the Last Man* (New York: the Free Press, 1992). Since Fukuyama's primary texts are Hegel's and Nietzsche's, we are clearly barking up the same trees. Were this a scholarly book (which it is not) and had there not been quarts of ink and reams of paper expended in response to Fukuyama (which there have), I would not be able to avoid a sustained discussion of my respect for and differences with Fukuyama's position. For my own foray into the dark wood of Hegel scholarship, see my "Reflections on the Absolute," *The Review of Metaphysics* 28, no. 3 (March 1975): 520–46. For a treatment of "the end of history" that pre-dates Fukuyama but remains both closer to Hegel and to our contemporary condition, see Mark Taylor, *Erring: A Postmodern A/theology* (Chicago: University of Chicago Press, 1984), especially chap. 3, "End of History," 52–73.

page 27: The epigram is from Nietzsche, *The Genealogy of Morals,* trans. Francis Golffing (Garden City, New York: Doubleday Anchor, 1956), 231 and 299.

page 41: Andre Breton, "Manifesto of Surrealism (1924)," in *Manifestoes of Surrealism,* trans. Richard Seaver and Helen Lane (Ann Arbor: University of Michigan Press, 1972), 47.

page 47: The epigram from Nietzsche is from *The Will to Power,* ed. and trans. Walter Kaufmann (New York: Vintage, 1968), p. 18, aphorism no. 25, from spring–fall 1887. Given the importance of this quotation for this book, there may be some who would like the German: *"Wenn man einem Ziele entgegengeht, so sheint es unmöglich, dass 'die Ziellosigkeit an sich' unser Glaubensgrundsatz ist."* Friedrich Nietzsche, *Werke in Drei Baenden,* ed. Karl Schlechta, vol. 3 (Munich: Carl Hanser Verlag, 1956), 530.

page 50: The national survey of the values of college freshmen are conducted under the directorship of Professor Alexander Astin at UCLA.

pages 55: On Heidegger and the Nazis see Victor Farias, *Heidegger et le Nazisme.* For a more thoughtful treatment of the subject, see Avital Ronell, *The Telephone Book* (Lincoln and London: University of Nebraska Press, 1989).

page 66: Jean-François Lyotard, *The Postmodern Condition: A Report on Knowledge,* trans. Geoff Bennington and Brian Massumi (Manchester: Manchester University Press, 1984). The literature on postmodernism grows more immense every day. Beginning with an early trickle of intimations reviewed in a careful and thorough book by Margaret Rose (*The Post-Modern and the Post-Industrial* [Cambridge: Cambridge University Press, 1991]), a stream of books and articles on art and architecture flowed from the fluent pen of Charles Jencks. Then the pace picked up with books of literary criticism and *theory,* for example, by Ihab Hassan (*The Postmodern Turn* [Athens, Ohio: Ohio University Press, 1987]), and on postmodernism and politics, for example, the anthology *Postmodernism and Politics,* ed. Jonathan Arac (Minneapolis: University of Minnesota Press, 1986); David Harvey, *The Condition of Postmodernity* (Oxford: Basil Blackwell, 1989); and Fredric Jameson, *Postmodernism, or, The Cultural Logic of Late Capitalism* (Durham: Duke University Press, 1991). I've done my best to tread water in this torrent with a long article, "This Postmodern Business," in *Marketing and Research Today,* February 1990, 4–22.

page 83: Norman Mailer, *Genius and Lust: A Journey Through the Major Writings of Henry Miller* (New York: Grove Press, 1976).

pages 85–86: Randall Reid, "Detritus," *New American Review 14:* 17f.

page 86: Roland Barthes, *Roland Barthes,* trans. Richard Howard (New York: Hill & Wang, 1977), 92ff., 99, 110, 143.

pages 87–88: G. W. F. Hegel, *The Phenomenology of Mind,* trans. Baillie (London: Allen & Unwin, 1931), 229.

page 93: Thomas Weiskel, *The Romantic Sublime: Studies in the Structure and Psychology of Transcendence* (Baltimore and London: Johns Hopkins University Press, 1976), 50.

page 101: Both quotes from John Keats, *Howard Hughes* (New York: Random House, 1966), 151, 198.

page 126: Sigmund Freud, *Civilization and its Discontents,* trans. James Strachey (New York: W. W. Norton & Company, 1961), 50f., 62.

page 129: Nietzsche, *op. cit.,* 317, aphorism no. 585.

page 141: Karl Marx, *Capital,* vol. 1 (New York: International Publishers, 1967), 467.

page 143: Friedrich Nietzsche, *Twilight of the Idols* (Baltimore: Penguin, 1968), 68: "Maxims and Arrows" #12.

page 170:   *Now I a fourfold vision see,*
And a fourfold vision is given to me;
'Tis fourfold in my supreme delight
And threefold in soft Beulah's night
And twofold Always. May God us keep
From Single vision and Newton's sleep!

William Blake, Letter to Butts, November 22, 1802; quoted in Norman O. Brown, *Love's Body* (New York: Vintage, 1966), 193.

page 175: Mary Catherine Bateson, *Composing a Life* (New York: Plume/Penguin, 1990), 4. The daughter's lovely book is clearly influenced by the father, with whom she was a close collaborator on *Angels Fear: Towards an Epistemology of the Sacred.* For an essay of Gregory Bateson's that started me down the road toward this book, see "Conscious Purpose versus Nature," in *Steps to an Ecology of Mind* (New York: Ballantine Books, 1972), 426–39.

page 183: Nietzsche sang of "The Blessed Isles" in *Thus Spoke Zarathustra,* pt. 2, sec. 2, in *Portable Nietzsche* (New York: Viking Penguin, 1977). For "wretched contentment," see Zarathustra's Prologue, sec. 3.

page 184: Georges Bataille, *The Accursed Share, vol. 1,* trans. Robert Hurley (New York: Zone Books, 1988), 37. The next quote from Bataille is from p. 33, and "elsewhere" refers to Bataille's "Letter to René Char on the Incompatibilities of the Writer," reprinted in *Yale French Studies* 78 (1990): 40.

page 185: The quotation from Jean Baudrillard is from *Revenge of the Crystal,* ed. and trans. Paul Foss and Juliann Pefanis (London, Concord, Mass.: Pluto Press, 1990), 105.

CURRENCY

DOUBLEDAY